VIRGINIA
LAND GRANTS

Virginia Land Grants

A STUDY OF CONVEYANCING IN RELATION TO COLONIAL POLITICS

Fairfax Harrison

HERITAGE BOOKS
2007

HERITAGE BOOKS

AN IMPRINT OF HERITAGE BOOKS, INC.

Books, CDs, and more—Worldwide

For our listing of thousands of titles see our website
at
www.HeritageBooks.com

A Facsimile Reprint
Published 2007 by
HERITAGE BOOKS, INC.
Publishing Division
65 East Main Street
Westminster, Maryland 21157-5026

Originally Privately Printed
The Old Dominion Press
Richmond
1925

International Standard Book Number: 978-1-888265-61-3

CONTENTS

INTRODUCTION

IN the Land Office at Richmond are preserved MS. books which constitute Virginia's most precious surviving muniment of her past. They are the records of the land grants in the Dominion from 1624 down to the American Revolution; in two series which, after 1690, are contemporaneous, viz: (1) The Land Patent Books kept by the Virginia government, and (2) The Northern Neck Grant Books kept by the proprietors of the Northern Neck.

These books are much more than fountains of land titles. Important as they remain on that account, they warrant study by the historian on others; for they are shot through, like Domesday Book, with veins of casual reference to local conditions; as witness Dr. Stanard's demonstration (in *Va. Mag.,* vols. i-vii) that the earliest of them are mines of topographical and genealogical source material.

Stimulated by Professor F. J. Turner's thesis (*The Frontier in American History*) that American democracy was not carried to Virginia in the *Susan Constant* but was developed there under the influence of frontier conditions, the chief of which was free land, the present study of these records was undertaken in the endeavor to throw light on a special historical problem, for which there are few political documents, and those few highly coloured by the passions aroused by Charles II's grant of Virginia to Lords Arlington and Culpeper.

The working hypothesis was that, as the two series of land grants overlap in the stripling margins of river plantations seated during the Commonwealth on the Potomac and the Rappahannock, a systematic comparison of the rival conveyancing practices against an historical background might yield an economic explanation of (1) the local resistance to, and (2) the ultimate acceptance of, the proprietors of the Northern Neck in that region.

The evidences so deduced are illuminating. They prove the dominant importance of the head-right in shaping the civilization of the colony and reveal the causes of the decay and atrophy of that institution; but most of all they suggest that further study of the documents may make it possible for the historian convincingly to carry back for several generations the origin of the political intransigence of Virginia in the eighteenth century. Developing Alexander Brown's thesis, it is easier to comprehend our ancestors resentment of a call to assume what in itself now seems, to their tax-ridden descendants, to have been not an undue share of the imperial burdens consequent upon the war with France, when it appears that, by iterated insistence upon a precedent established by the Virginia Company, the colony had, for more than a century prior to 1765, successfully fended off all attempts of the Crown to revoke its original surrender of those two fundamentals of sovereignty, the control of the creation of land titles and the measure of land taxes.

F. H.

Belvoir,
Fauquier County, Virginia.
December, 1924.

CHAPTER ONE

The Land Patent Books

§ 1. *The Constitution of the Virginia Commonwealth.*

THE peculiar interest of the colonial Virginia land title lies in the fact that the entire territory was originally vested in a commercial Company which declared that every member who contributed to the settlement or development of the colony thereby became entitled to a dividend out of a common stock of land. Although the Crown soon ousted the Company and took over the political government, that action was followed by recognition not only of the property rights of the members of the Company who had already perfected their dividends by securing individual grants of land, but of the principle that those who thereafter qualified on the terms the Company had laid down became likewise entitled to similar 'dividends.'

Virginia was thus in her origin a true Commonwealth. She acquired, and thereafter tenaciously held and exercised, the collective franchise herself to dispose of lands on a steadily widening frontier. Every newcomer to her shores was taught that he was, by the mere fact of immigration, vested with a reserved legal right sooner or later to carve an individual holding out of the inexhaustible abundance of land which lay back of whatever seatings had already been made. It is only by understanding that this sense of a 'right' to the 'waste' had become implicit in the colonial character and had profoundly modified the inherited notions of property in land which the immigrant had brought with him out of the long settled civilization of England, that one can now appreciate the passion with which seventeenth century Virginians cherished the head right as an 'antient priviledge.' It is thus, and thus only, that one can interpret the emphasis put on the preservation of it in the capitulation to the Parliament at the beginning of 1652, and in the charter secured from Charles II in 1676.

The conspicuous fact about the Virginia land system was, then, that a land grant was never accepted as a grace of royalty. In the eighteenth century, when the British government and the royal Governors were increasingly alert to assert the prerogative of the Crown in relation to the colonies, an altered form of patent did, indeed, give it somewhat that appearance, incidentally glossing over the original plain recital of the origin of the franchise on which it was based; but even then there still remained in use apt words which served historically to declare the unaltered fact that the Virginia planter was a member of a community which had once been a corporation and as such had inherited a 'right' to a 'dividend' of land.[1]

In practice, this assurance extended to a crystallization of the nominal terms on which land was acquired and held. The 'fee rent' which the Company reserved as a mere badge of the feudal tenure on which it had taken its own charter title, was, under its other and more comfortable technical name of 'quit rent,' maintained without increase in amount as the measure of all land taxes, even under conditions widely different from those which obtained when it was first prescribed. Moreover, when immigration ceased to be the chief test of an adventure in the colony, the principle of the 'dividend' held in equilibrium the value at which the head right was commuted. No suggestion of the increased cost of living of government, or even of the enhancing value of land was permitted to vary these charges until the end of the colonial period. In the high years of Virginia's prosperity before the French war of 1754 a purely incidental tax on the dividend, as petty in amount as Dinwiddie's 'pistole fee,' was doggedly resisted as involving a principle; it was only a pressing need of revenue for self defense in the life and death struggle against France that persuaded the Assembly, after first stretching the normal poll tax to its elastic limit, to levy, in 1755, a tax on land. How distasteful was this unprecedented measure is apparent in the travail which preceded its birth and in its repeal as soon as the crisis had passed.

It followed that, while in Maryland and Pennsylvania, where the planters had no such history behind them, the proprietors steadily increased the cost of acquiring and holding land,[2] in Virginia the basis of that cost remained, until 1755, what it had been under the Company in 1618; nor were the people of the Northern Neck deprived of a share of this inheritance, for there the practical consideration of competition with the Virginia land office limited any attempt by Lord Fairfax's agents to follow the example of the Penns and the Calverts.

If, for such considerations, colonial Virginia cherished her land laws, it is of as curious interest that descendants of Virginia planters should boast of holding lands 'given' to their ancestors 'by King George,' as it is that a franchise, achieved not without dust and heat, should be withdrawn, as it was by the land act of 1779,[3] only when the colony discarded allegiance to the Crown and set up a popular government.

In the exercise of this franchise there were three alternative methods by which colonial Virginians could, and did, initiate individual land titles. They were summed up in the act of 1779, just referred to, by which the revolutionary government set up its own administrative machinery for dealing with 'waste lands.' Here were declared good and valid

'all surveys of waste and unappropriated land . . . founded either upon
'*charter importation rights* duly proved and certified according to ancient usage . . . or upon
'*treasury rights* for money paid to the receiver general . . . or upon
'*military service* in virtue of any proclamation either from the King of Great Britain or any former governor of Virginia.'

Although most of the titles perfected in the seventeenth

century were based on the importation or 'head' right, and
most of those perfected in the eighteenth century on the 'treasury' right, all three rights were available from the beginning
of the colony down to the revolution of 1776, and every patent
in the books we are studying may be referred to one or the
other of them. After a preliminary examination of the sources
of them all they will, accordingly, be considered in turn.

By his charter of 1606 James I granted Virginia to Sir
Thomas Gates and associates, and agreed with them

> 'by letters patent under the great seal of England [to]
> give and grant unto such persons, their heirs and assigns, as
> the Council of that colony . . . shall for that purpose
> nominate and assign, all the lands . . . which shall be
> within the precincts limited for that colony, as is aforesaid, to
> be holden of us, our heirs and successors, as of our manor of
> East Greenwich in the county of Kent in free and common
> soccage only, and not in capite.'[4]

Thus was established the legal status of the future private
rights.

By the Second Charter (1609) the patentees were 'incorporated by the name of The Treasurer and Company of Adventurers and Planters of the City of London for the first
Colony in Virginia,' and were authorized themselves:

> 'under their common seal [to] distribute, convey, assign
> . . . such particular portions of lands . . . unto
> such our loving subjects, naturally born, or denizens or others,
> as well adventurers as planters as by the said company . . .
> shall be nominated, appointed or allowed.'[5]

Under this authority the Company at once put out its tract,
Nova Britannia,[6] in which was outlined the land law which
was to obtain in Virginia down to the American Revolution,
as follows, viz:

> 'We call those Planters that goe in their persons to dwell
> there: and those Adventurers that adventure their money and

go not in person, and both doe make the members of one Colonie. We do account twelve pounds ten shillings to be a single share adventured. Every ordinary man or woman, if they will goe and dwell there, and every child above tenne yeares that shall be carried thither to remaine shall be allowed for each of their persons a single share, as if they had adventured twelve pounds ten shillings in money . . .

'All charges of setling and maintaining the Plantacon and of making supplies shall be borne in a joint stock of the adventurers for seven yeares after the date of our new enlargement [i. e., the second charter of 1609] during which time there shall be no adventure nor goods returned in private from thence, neytheir by Master, Marriner, Planter nor Passenger, they shall be restrained by bond and search that as we supplie from hence to the Planters at our owne charge all necessaries for food and apparel for fortifying and building of houses in a joynt stock, so they are to returne from thence the increase and fruits of their labours, for the use and advancement of the same joynt stock, till the end of seven yeares: at which time we propose (God willing) to make a division by Commissioners appointed to all the lands graunted unto us by his Majestie, to every of the Colonie according to each man's several adventure, agreeing with our Register book, which wee doubt not will bee for every share of twelve pounds tenne shillings, five hundred acres at least . . .

'Assuredly after the second yeare the returnes from thence will be able with an over plus to make supplies at large, so that our purses shall be freed, and the over plus of stock will also grow to greatness, which stock is also (as the land) to be divided equally at seven yeares end or sooner, or so often as the Company shall thinke fit for the greatness of it to make a Divident.'

When the seven years expired in which it had so been stipulated that all lands and other property in the colony should remain in 'common stock,' the Company had completed the painful period of the crepuscular effort to plant a colony. The adventurers had borne a loss of at least £20,000, and the planters had dedicated many lives. Some of the adventurers, looking only for present gain, had meanwhile abandoned their investment, 'bidding it aidiew and never looked after it again.' Others who had subscribed with promise to pay in installments, 'had paid the first paiment but refuse to pay the rest;'

but the high emprise was kept alive by the few who 'to their praise, from the first undertaking to this day have not ceased to give their counsels, spend their times and lay down their monies.' These few, being in control, under the leadership of Sir Thomas Smythe, now made an appeal for new subscriptions and, to induce them, voted at once to carry out the plan of 1609 for dividends of land. In their *Brief Declaration,* published in April, 1616, it was announced that:

'We intend, God willing, to beginne a present Division, by Lot, to every man that hath already adventured his money or person, for every single share of twelve pounds tenne shillings, fifty Acres of Land till further opportunitie will afford to divide the rest, which we doubt not will bring at least two hundred acres to every single share.

'This Division is intended to be done by a new Governor [Argall] with Commissioners and surveyors to be sent from hence to joyne with others that are there already, to give every man his Lot in due proporcon, according to such indifferent Directions as shall be given them in charge .   .   .

'And furthermore, every man's portion allotted to him shall be confirmed as an estate of inheritance to him and his heyers forever, with bounds and limits, under the Company's seale, to be holden of his Maiestie, as of his Manour of East Greenwich, in Socage Tenure, and not in capite, according to his Maiesties gracious Letters Patents already granted to the Virginia Company in that behalfe.'

But as more funds were at once necessary, there was levied an assessment equivalent to one new share (£12, 10s.) upon all adventurers who wished to participate in the dividend of lands.

On these terms a number of adventurers came forward and claimed their dividends, and land grants were duly voted to them by the Company. The earliest of them of which the record survives, and probably the first individual land title created in Virginia, was that vested on March 6, 1615/16, in Simon Codrington.

Contemporaneously with this announcement Governor Argall reached Virginia and superseded Sir Thomas Dale. The Company subsequently recorded that, 'by the singular Industry and virtue of . . . Sir Thomas Dale the former Difficulties and Dangers were in greatest part overcome, to the great ease and security of such as have been since that time transported thither,'

and in consequence 'the coming away of Sir Thomas Dale' in April, 1616, has ever since been held to mark the end of the doubtful period of the colony. The immediate consequence was that the Company now turned to maturing Sir Edwin Sandys' long nursed ambition to create a self-governing Commonwealth, 'the first Republic in America.' The results of the protracted deliberations to that end were formulated at the Quarter Court held on November 18, 1618, when were voted the ever memorable *Orders and Constitutions*. These resolutions of a commercial Company were in effect a state paper for they constituted what the first legislative Assembly held in America, summoned to consider them in 1619, called, without exaggeration, 'the Great Charter of privileges, orders and laws.'[7]

In this Magna Carta of 1618 provision was made first of a frame of local government and then of a complete and well rounded plan for the division of lands. In the latter respect it was ordained:

1. That the existing plantations on James River should be divided, for purposes of administration, into 'four cities or Boroughs, namely the chief city called James Town, Charles City, Henrico and the Borough of Kiccotan.'

2. That in each of these corporations there should first be set aside areas of common lands sufficient to support the magistracy, the church, and the proposed college: the interesting and laudable intent of the appropriations being declared to be 'to ease all the Inhabitants of Virginia forever of all Taxes and public burthens as may be, and to take away all occasion of oppression and corruption.'

3. That the existing members of the Company, both adventurers and planters who had not yet received their dividends, should then have lands laid off to them according to the number of their shares. The basis prescribed was 100 acres per share, of which 50 acres should be at once allotted and the remaining 50 should be allotted at such time in the future as

the expanded area of the colony should admit. To this, however, was attached a proviso that the 'ancient' members should
in all cases have twice the acreage of those who had come in
'since the coming away of Sir Thomas Dale.'

Having thus provided for the past, the Orders and Constitutions proceeded to lay down the constitutional principle
that 'the Governor for the time being and the said Council of
State'[8] should always have power to allot lands in the future,
thus making provision for those who increased their interest
in the Company and for new members, both adventurers and
planters. Thereby were established the 'treasury right' and
the 'head right,' which the Revolutionary Assembly recognised
in 1779.

After the Crown took over the affairs of the colony in
the summer of 1624, it tacitly suffered the royal Governors to
continue to make grants in perfection of individual rights already accrued under the Company, but it is apparent from
the documents that the Privy Council was for a time at a loss
for a policy in respect to the further disposition of waste
lands. In the end this hesitation operated to the advantage of
the planter, so that to it may be attributed a substantial part
of the subsequent colonial opposition to the revival of the
Company. No attempt was made by Charles I to open a
Crown office for the sale of lands and, as a consequence, the
Company's 'treasury right' was suspended as a working principle until 1699, when, under new conditions, it was revived.
On the other hand, the Crown did, within a few years, renew
the immigration or 'head' right, and left its administration to
the local government, as we shall now proceed to show.

§ 2. *The Head Right*

Virginia's Magna Carta of 1618, looking to the future,
provided:

'That for all persons . . . which during the next
seven years after Midsummer day, 1618, shall go into Virginia
with intent there to inhabit, if they continue there three years

or dye after they are shipped, there shall be a Grant made of fifty acres for every person, upon a first division and as many more upon a second division (the first being peopled), which grants are to be made respectively to such persons and their heirs at whose charges the said persons going to inhabit in Virginia shall be transported: with reservation of Twelve pence yearly rent for every fifty acres, to be answered to the said Treasurer and Company and their Successors, after the first Seven Years of every such grant.'

The land patent devised to give effect to this franchise determined all the forms subsequently used for that purpose down to the American Revolution. The earliest surviving example of it was a grant, made January 26, 1621/2, by Sir Francis Wyatt to Thomas Hothersall, of 200 acres at Blunt Point, in what became Warwick County, viz:[9]

[Wyatt's form, under the Company]

By the Governr and Capt: Generll: of Virginia

To all to whome these prsents shall come greeting in our Lord God Everlasting.

Know Yee that I sr Francis Wyatt Kt, Governr and Capt: Generall of Virginia, by vertue of the great Charter of Orders and Lawes concluded on and dated at London in a Generall quarter Court the Eighteenth day of November One Thousand six hundred and Eighteene by the Treasurer Counseil and Company of Adventurers for the first Southerne Colony of Virginia, according to the Authority graunted them from his Matie under his great Seale, the said Charter being directed to the Governr and Counseil of State here resident, and by the rules of Justice, Equity & reason, doe wth the approbation and Consent of the same Counseil who are Joyned in Commission with mee, Give and graunt unto Mr. Thomas Hothersall of Paspehay gent., and to his heires and assignes for ever, for his first Generll: devident, to bee augmented and doubled by the said Company to him and his said heires and assignes when hee or they shall once sufficiently have planted and peopled the same,

Two hundrd acres of Land scituate and being at Blunt Point, Confining on the East the Land of Cornelius May, on the South upon the great River, on the North upon the Maine Land and on the West runing towards a small creek one hundred rod (at sixteene foote and a half the Rod);

Fifty acres whereof is his owne psonall Right and fifty acres is the psonall Right of Frances Hothersall his wife, the other hundred

acres in consideration of his transportacon of twoe of his Children out
of England at his owne cost & Charges, Viz: Richard Hothersall and
Mary Hothersall,

To Have and to Hold the said twoe hundred acres of Land wth
all and singular the apptennces, and wth his due share of all Mines
& Minneralls therein conteyned, and wth all rights and privileges of
hunting, hawking and fowling and others within the prcincts and upon
the borders of the said Land, To the only pper Use benifitt and behoofe of the said Thomas Hothersall, his heires and assignes for ever,

In as large and ample manner to all intents and purposes as is
specified in the said great Charter or by Consequence may justly bee
Collected out of the same, or out of his Ma'ties Letters Patents whereon
it is grounded.

Yeilding and paying to the Treasurer and Company and to their
Successors for ever, yearely at the feast of St. Michael the Archangell [September 29], for every fifty acres, the fee rent of one Shilling.

In Witness Whereof I have to these presents sett my hand and the
Great Seale of the Colony, Given at James Citty the six and twentieth
day of January one thousand six hundred twenty one [o. s.] and in
the yeares of the Raigne of our Soveraigne Lord, James by the Grace
of God King of England, Scotland, France and Ireland, Defender of
the faith &c., Vizt: of England, France and Ireland the Nineteenth
and of Scotland the five and fiftieth, and in the fifteenth yeare of this
Plantacon.

Governor Wyatt continued to issue head right patents in
this form to and including one of January 20, 1624/5.[10] Before another was ready for action by the Council, the good
ship *Anne* arrived in James River, bringing the great news
that on the June 24th preceding the Company had been dis-
solved by writ of *quo warranto*, that James I had assumed
the government and had issued to Wyatt, on August 26, 1624,
the first commission of a royal Governor of Virginia.[11] In this
commission there was nothing said about land grants. For all
that the Governor and Council were empowered generally to
govern

'as fullye and amplye as any Governor and Council resident there at any time within the space of five years now last
past had or might perform or execute,'

Wyatt issued no more patents prior to his leaving the colony in May, 1626. In that respect it appears, in the old phrase, *curia advisari vult.*

On March 27, 1625, James I died, and, on May 13th following, his successor, as Charles I, issued the famous proclamation declaring his policy with respect to Virginia.[12] Herein it was made known that the voiding of the company's charter by 'our most dear father of blessed memory,'

'was not intended by him to take away or impeach the particular interest of any private planter or adventurer, nor to alter the same otherwise than should be of necessity for the good of the public,'

but again nothing specific was said as to land grants. The established planters were, in consequence, left somewhat in the air, while newcomers thought of returning to England. The Council accordingly sent Sir George Yeardley to England to represent their plight, particularly to secure, if possible, a definite confirmation of the lands already vested and, whatever the future might hold, an assurance of those rights which had already accrued but were not yet perfected by dividends. Yeardley's embassy seemed to drag and uncertainty spelled increasing difficulty in the colony. It was perhaps for this reason that Wyatt now asked permission to leave his government, as, by reason of the death of the Governor's father, James I had already agreed that he might. But before a response could be received to this request, in a dispatch of April 6, 1626, Wyatt again represented to the Privy Council the situation of the planters:

'The King's assurance,' he said,[13] 'that every man shall have his particular right preserved and enlarged will be the means of inviting many to settle who hitherto have only endeavored a present crop and their hasty return.'

These representations had only a limited effect. To relieve Wyatt personally there was issued, on March 14, 1625/6, a commission to Yeardley, as Governor.[14] The powers authorized were in the identical general language of Wyatt's commission, and they were supplemented by instructions of April 19, 1626, which again temporized with the problem of 'waste lands.'[15] No more was provided than:

'that all newcomers be well entertained and lodged, and if [they] be unprovided of land fit to manure they [are] to be permitted to sit down upon the Company's land upon the conditions expressed in the Treas[r] and Council's letter sent, immediately after the massacre, in August, 1622.'

Yeardley arrived in Virginia at the end of May, 1626, and found, as doubtless he had anticipated, that his powers were by no means what the planters expected. The record is lacking, but he must have made new representations and have received permission to assuage the situation by interpreting his commission as power to issue patents in respect of such head rights, accrued prior to the dissolution of the Company, as Wyatt had not perfected. At all events, in February, 1626/7, be began, and thenceforth until his death in November, 1627, continued, to issue patents to planters who were in the colony in 1624 in a form of which the following is an example,[16] viz:

[Yeardley's form, under the King's commission]

By the Governr: and Capt. Generll: of Virginia:
To all to whome these Pr'sents shall come, greeting in our Lord God Everlasting.

Whereas by the ordinances and constitutions made & sett forth by the late Company it is ordered and appointed that such lands & devidents as shall bee due to any Adventurers or planters, of what Condicon or quality soever they bee, should bee laid out and assigned unto them by the Governr. and Councell here established,

And whereas the same power & authoritie is confirmed and graunted by his Maj'ties Letters Pattents directed unto mee and the Councell of State bearing date the fowerteenth day of March one Thousand six hundred twenty and five [O. S.]

Now Know Yee that I Sr. George Yeardly &c. doe with the Consent of the Councell of State give and grant Unto Capt. William Epes of Accomacke and to his heires and assignee forever

Fower hundred and fifty acres of Land as his first devident & Upon a second devision to bee augmented and doubled unto him his said heires & assignee when hee or they shall sufficiently have peopled and planted the same,

Scituate and being on the Easterne shoare of the Bay of Chese-peiacke and lying neare unto the plantacon of Accomacke and abutting Northerly on the Mouth of the Creeke comonly called by the name of the Kings Creeke, parting the same from the land belonging to the place of [the] Secretary and thence extending Southerly twoe hundred five and twenty pole towards the pursimond ponds, Easterly upon the banke along the shore of the said Bay of Chesepeyacke, and Westerly extending directly into the maine Land

The said fower hundred and fifty acres accrewing by Vertue of the transportacon of nine men into this Country (Vitz:) William Jones, William Gallaway, John Barker, Edward Rogers and Thomas Warden, whoe all arrived in the *Anne* 1623, and Nicholas Raynbeare who arrived in the *Swann* in 1624, and Henry Carter whoe arrived in the *James* 1624, and assigned over unto him by William Streats Mar-riner, and Richard Reene and John Robins whoe arrived in the *Returne* 1625.

To Have and to Hold the said fower hundred and fifty acres of land with the apptennces, and with his due share of all Mines and Min-neralls therein conteyned and with all rights and priviledges of hunt-ing, fishing, fowling and others within the pr'incts and upon the borders of the same, to the sole and pper. Use benefitt and behoofe of him the said Capt. William Epes, his said heires and assignes for ever.

In as large and ample manner to all intents and purposes as is ex-pressed in the said Ordinances and Conditions or by Consequence may bee justly Collected out of the same or out of his Maj'ties Letters Pattents whereon they are grounded.

Yielding and paying for every fifty acres of land herein by these prsents given and graunted, yearly at the feast of St. Michaell the Arch-angell [September 29], the fee rent of one shilling.

Provided that if the said Capt. William Epes, his heires or assignes shall not plant & seate Upon the said fower hundred and fifty acres of Land with in the time and terme of three yeares now next ensuing the date hereof, That then itt shall and may bee Lawfull for any Ad-venturer or planter to make choice and seate there upon the same.

In Witness Whereof I have hereunto sett my hand and the Seale of the Colony, Given at James Citty the third day of February in the second yeare of the raigne of our Soveraigne Lord Charles, King, &c., Anno. dom. one Thousand six hundred twenty six [O. S.], Col. Virga, the XXth.

After Yeardley's death, Francis West and John Pott, the successive Presidents, who were elected by the Council in pur-suance of the authority provided for such an emergency by Yeardley's commission, and who maintained the government until Harvey arrived in the spring of 1630, continued the practice of satisfying the claims of the ancient planters. West followed Yeardley's patent form in so many words, but Pott (for what reason does not appear) substituted for the recital of royal authority a vague, and, as compared with Wyatt's patents a greatly abbreviated, rehearsal of the Orders and Constitutions of 1618, viz:

[Dr. Pott's form]

'Whereas by the Orders and Constitutions formerly made and established for the affairs of this Colony it hath beene ordayned and appointed that all devidents of lands anyway due or belonging to any Adventurers & Planters of what condicon soever should bee laid out and assigned to them according to the condicons in the same menconed.'

In Yeardley's commission of 1626, the next reversion of the governorship had been assured to that robustious sea captain, John Harvey. When the news of Yeardley's death reached England, a commission was accordingly issued to Harvey under date of March 26, 1628.[17] This was in the now familiar general form held by the previous Governors, but a step forward in the history of the head right franchise was recorded in the instructions which, on September 12, 1628,[18] supplemented the commission, viz:

'First wee doe hereby declare and promise to take these Collonies of our Subjects in Virginia into our royall protection.
'Wee doe likewise promise hereby to renew and confirm unto the said Collonies under our greate Seal of England their landes and priviledges formerlie graunted.'

Being in the naval service and engaged in the several fruitless fleet operations of Charles I's wars with Spain and France, Harvey postponed his departure for Virginia until after the murder of his patron, 'Steenie,' Duke of Buckingham. At last, in August, 1629, he prepared to take up his government. His previous experience in the colony taught him what an asset he would have if he could take with him a definite authority to realize the royal promise of the preceding year, and he then re-opened the question of land titles. As Harvey has not left a savory reputation in Virginia history, it is only fair to give him credit where it is due. There can be no doubt that it was his persistence which finally secured the recognition by the Crown of the head right as a working principle. A surviving paper of propositions made to the Privy Council and annotated with comments by an anonymous committee shows that in 1629 the Crown was not yet ready to carry out that promise and, indeed, expected to deal with the grant of lands in detail at home. Harvey represented:[19]

'2. That his Matie wil be pleased gratiously to extend his favour to the planters for a confirmation of their lands and goods by charter under the greate Seal of England,'

and in response it was noted,

'2. The setling of lands and goods and priviledges is to be done here, and may be done by calling in the former books and charters at a convenient time.'

And so when Harvey reached Virginia in 1630 he had no more authority as to land grants than his immediate predecessors. He continued to perfect the dividends of the ancient planters and, indeed, taking a chance, ventured to issue some patents, based on head rights accrued since the dissolution of the Company.[20] In doing so he used two forms. Some of his patents were in Dr. Pott's form (which probably represented dividends for which the papers had been drafted while Pott was still acting Governor), but the greater number of Harvey's early patents were in Yeardley's form, substituting only in the recital of authority the date of his own commission (March 26, 1628) for that of his predecessor (March 14, 1625/6).[21]

During this period the fate of the head right was trembling in the balance. There was on foot in England an active and hopeful lobby seeking to reinstate the Company, or, in the alternative, there was the possibility that the colony might be subjected to some other form of proprietary government. In either event, Virginia deemed that there would be an immediate hazard in respect to land titles accrued since 1625, if not to those of older date, while the local administration of the head right, which was of the essence of the franchise, might be suspended. The anxiety of the planters in this situation to button up what they had achieved is patent in their willingness to abate the full measure of their expectations. On February 21, 1631/2,[22] a year after Harvey had assumed his post, he joined the Council in a new memorial to the Crown, praying:

'That we may have confirmation of all our lands and dividents, and that they which have arived since the 24th of June, 1625, to which tyme all comers were to have fifty acres of land, may likewise have a pporcon graunted unto them; which we desire may be 25 acres, and for encouragement to after comers we wsh also that 12 acres may bee graunted unto all such as shall come during the terme of 7 years next ensuinge.'

Again, after Maryland had been erected and Virginia had her first shiver of realization of a Lord Proprietor established within her charter domain, Harvey wrote again, on February 7, 1633/4:[23]

'The inhabitants are importunate for a confirmation of their lands and privileges promised by the King, by reason of the grant to Lord Baltimore.'

This last appeal was effective. If the loss of Maryland had accomplished no other good, it secured to Virginia the assurance of the head right. On July 22, 1634,[24] the Privy Council sent Harvey a dispatch which vouchsafed more than the planters had been willing in their anxiety to accept by way of compromise:

'We have thought fit to certify you that his Majesty of his royal favor, and for the better encouragement of the planters there doth let you knowe that it is not intended that the interestes which men had settled when you were a Corporation should be impeached; that for the present they may enjoy their estates and trades with the same freedom and privileges as they did before the recalling of their Patents: To which purpose also in pursuance of his Majesty's gracious intention, wee doe hereby authorize you to dispose of such proportions of Lands to all those planters beeing freemen as you had power to doe before the yeare 1625.'

Upon this the patent form was changed again, and during the remainder of Harvey's first term, including the few patents issued by Capt. John West after the 'thrusting out' on April 28, 1635, the following form was used,[25] viz:

[Harvey's second form, after the royal confirmation of the head right]

To all to whome these prsents. shall come, I Sr. John Harvey Kt. Governr. and Capt. Generll. of Virginia send greeting in our Lord God Everlasting.

Whereas by Letters Pattents bearing date the twoe and twentieth of July one Thousand six hundred thirtie fower from the Rt. Honble. the Lords of his Majties. most Honoble. Privie Councell their Lordshipps did authorize the Governr. and Councell of Virginia to dispose of such pportions of land to all planters being freemen as they had power to doe before the yeare 1625, whence according to divers orders & Constitutions in that case provided and appointed all devidents of Lands any waies due or belonging to any Adventurers or planters o f what condicon soever were to bee laid out and assigned unto them according to the severall Condicons in the same menconed.

Now Know Yee therefore that I the said Sr. John Harvey doe with the consent of the Councell of State give and graunt unto Capt. Hugh Bullocke and to his heires and assignes for ever by these prsents Twoe Thousand five hundred and fiftie acres of land, scituate, lying & being from the runn that falleth downe by the Eastern side of a peece of land knowne by the name of the Woodyard and soe from that runn along the side of the Pocoson (or great Otter pond soe called) Northwest and about the head of the said Otter pond back Southeast leaveing the Otter pond in the middle.

To have and to Hold the said twoe Thousand five hundred and fiftie acres of land with his due share of all Mines and Minneralls therein Conteyned and with all rights and priviledges of hunting, hawking, fishing and fowling, wth in the prcincts of the same to the sole and pper Use benifitt and behoofe of him the said Capt. Bullocke his heires and assignes for ever.

In as large and ample manner to all intents and purposes as is expressed in the said orders and Constitutions, or by Consequence may bee justly Collected out of the same or out of his Majties. Letters Pattents whereon they are grounded.

Yielding and paying for every fiftie acres of land herein by these presents given and graunted yearely at the feast of St. Michaell the Archangell [September 29], the fee rent of one shilling to his Majties. Use.

Provided always that [if] the said Capt. Hugh Bullock, his heires or assignes shall not plant or seate or cause to bee planted on the said twoe Thousand five hundred & fiftie acres of land wth in the time and terme of three yeares now next ensuing the date hereof, that then it shall and may bee lawfull for any Adventurer or planter to make Choice and seate upon the same.

Given at James Citty under my hand and sealed with the seale of the Colony the twelfth day of March one Thousand six hundred thirtie fower [O. S.] & in the tenth year of our Soveraigne Lord King Charles &c.

After Harvey returned to Virginia in January, 1636/7, with his new commission, dated April 2, 1636,[26] and the accompanying instructions, dated on the May 22nd following,[27] he altered the recital of his authority to make land grants to read as follows:[28]

[Harvey's third form, under his commission of 1636]

'*Whereas* by Instructions from the King's Most Excellent Majtie, directed to mee and the Councell here resident, bearing date the 22nd of May in the twelfth Yeare of his Majties Raigne, His Majtie was gratiously pleased, for the better encouragement of all Adventurers and planters, to authorize and Command us to give and assigne to all freemen such pporcons of Lands as were heretofore given and graunted unto the planters being freemen of this Colony.'

It will be noted that in his two last forms Harvey based his authority entirely on the will of the Crown, but so long as the government at home did not interfere in the detailed administration this was a merely formal defect so far as Virginia was concerned. The franchise remained intact by reason of the Crown's recognition of it.

The principle of the head right was thus settled. The authority to succeeding Governors to make land grants in pursuance of it became routine. Thus the instructions of January, 1638/9, to Wyatt[29] and of August, 1641, to Berkeley,[30] contained specific recognition of it in identical language, as follows:

'That you shall have power to grant Patents and to assign such Proportion of Land to all adventurers and Planters as have been usual heretofore in the like cases, either for adventurers of money [or] Transportation of people thither, according to the orders of the late Company, and since allowed by his Majesty. And that there likewise be the same proportion of Fifty acres of land granted and assigned for every person transported thither since Midsummer, 1625, And that you continue the same course to all persons transported thither until it shall be otherwise determined by his Majesty.'

In view of Harvey's suppression of a reference to the Orders and Constitutions of 1618, the form of patent used by his successors from 1639 to 1652, which followed the language of their instructions, has the significance of renewing the memory of the origin of the head right. That form was as follows :[31]

[Berkeley's form prior to the Commonwealth]

To all to whom these presents shall come, I, Sir Wm. Berkeley, Knight, Governor and Captain-General of Virginia, send greeting in our Lord God everlasting:

Whereas, by the instruction from the King's most excellent Majesty, directed to me and the Council of State, his Majesty was graciously pleased to authorize me, the said Governor and Council, to grant patents, and to assign such proportions of land, to all adventurers and planters as have been usual heretofore in the like case, either for adventurers of money or transportation of people into the Colony, according to a charter of orders from the late Treasurer and Company; and that these be the same proportions of fifty acres of land granted and assigned for every person that hath been transported hither since midsummer, 1625; and that the same course be continued to all adventurers and planters until it shall be otherwise determined by his Majesty;

Now Know Ye that I, the said Sir Wm. Berkeley, do, with the advice and consent of the Council of State, accordingly give and grant unto . . . acres of land lying and being in the county of . . .

The said land being due unto the said . . . by and for the transportation of . . . persons into the colony, all whose names are, in record, mentioned under this patent.

To Have and to Hold the said land with his due share of all mines and minerals therein contained; with all rights and privileges of hunting, hawking, fishing and fowling; with all woods, waters and rivers; with all profits, commodities and hereditaments whatsoever in any wise

belonging, unto him the said . . . his heirs and assigns forever, in
as large and ample manner, to all intents and purposes, as is expressed
in a charter of orders from the late Treasurer and Company, dated the
18th of November, 1618, or by consequence may be justly collected out
of the same, or out of the letters patent whereon they are grounded.

To be held of our Sovereign Lord the King, his heirs or successors
for ever, as of his manor of East Greenwich, in free and common
soccage, and not in capite nor by Knight's service,

Yielding and Paying unto our said Sovereign Lord the King, his
heirs and successors, for every fifty acres of land herein by these
[presents] given and granted, yearly at the feast of St. Michael the
Archangel [September 29], the fee rent of one shilling to his Majesty's
use

(which payment is to be made seven years after the date hereof
and not before, according to the said charter of orders and since confirmed by his Majesty's letter of instructions, as also by act of Assembly of the second of March, 1642.) [32]

Provided that if the said , . . his heirs or assigns, do not plant
or seat, or cause to be planted or seated, upon the said land within three
years next ensuing that then it may and shall be lawful for any adventurer or planter to make choice and seat thereupon.

Given at James Citty under my hand and the seal of the Colony
this . . . day of . . .

So it was that when Virginia capitulated to the Commonwealth in March, 1651/2, the head right was so well established
and cherished an institution that it was carefully reserved in
the articles,[33] as follows:

'5thly. That all the pattents of land granted under the
collony seale, by any of the precedent Governors, shall be and
remaine in their full force and strength.

'6thly. That the priviledge of haveing ffiftie acres of
land for every person transported in the collony shall continue
as formerly granted.'

In the exercise of this right the Governors elected by the
Assembly during the Commonwealth continued to make land
grants, using an adapted form, viz:[34]

[The Commonwealth form]

To all to whom these presents shall come, I . . . Governour
and Captain Generall of Virginia, send greeting in our Lord God everlasting:

Whereas by the Articles dated at James City the twelfth of March, one thousand six hundred fifty one [O. S.] concluded and signed by the Commissioners appointed by authority of Parliament for the reducing, settling and governing of Virginia, it was provided that the privilege of fifty acres of land for every person transported into the Colony should be continued as previously granted, and

Whereas by act of a Grand Assembly made the twenty-first of April one thousand six hundred fifty-two ([35]) it was provided that all patents shall hereafter be signed under the Governour's hand, with the Secretary's authoritie, and shall be accompted authentique and valid in law until a Colonie Seal shall be provided and appointed,

Now Know Ye, that I, the said . . ., in the name of the Keeper of the Liberties of England, by authority of Parliament and with consent of the Council of State do give and grant unto . . . acres of land situate . . . The said land being due to the said . . . by and for the transportation of . . . persons into the Colony, all whose names are in record mentioned under this patent.

To Have and to Hold the said land with its due share of all mines and minerals therein contained, with all rights and privileges of hunting, hawking, fishing and fowling, with all woods, waters and rivers; with all profits, commodities and hereditaments whatsoever in any wise belonging to the said land.

To him, the said . . . his heirs and assigns forever in as large and ample manner to all intents and purposes as is in a Charter of Orders from the late Treasurer and Company, dated the 18th of November, 1618, or by consequence may be justly collected out of the same or out of the letters patent on which the same are grounded.

Yielding and Paying to the rent gatherers thereto appointed, for every fifty acres of land herein by these presents given and granted, yearly, at the feast of St. Michael the Archangel [September 29], the fee rent of one shilling.

Which payment is to be made seven years after the first grant or seating thereof and not before.

Provided that if the said . . . his heirs or assigns does not plant or seat, or cause to be planted or seated the said land within three years next ensuing, that then it shall and may be lawful for any adventurer or planter to make choice and seat thereupon.

Given at James Citty this . . . day of . . . one thousand six hundred . . .

It is fair to assume that upon his reinstatement as royal Governor Berkeley (and his deputy, Francis Moryson) resumed and thenceforth, until after his return from England with Charles II's new instructions of September 12, 1662, practised his own earlier patent form, but, lacking an example, the proof is not available. As it happens, despite his criticism of the condition in which his predecessor, William Claiborne, had left the land books,[36] Secretary Thomas Ludwell consistently abbreviated his own land records by omitting all the formal parts of the patents, substituting for them that favorite phrase of the lazy clerk, *ut in aliis.*

Berkeley's instructions of 1662[37] necessitated, however, a material modification of both the Commonwealth and the ante-Commonwealth form of patent. They duly confirmed the head right, but, in doing so, revoked

'the grant of our Royal Father of blessed memory heretofore made to this our colony, to exempt the Planters from paying quit rent for the first seven years,'

because that exemption

'hath turned to the great prejudice of that our colony, and that many have abused that grace and taken occasion thereby to take and create a title to themselves of such Quantity of land which they never intend to, or in truth can, occupy or cultivate, but thereby only keep out others who would plant and manure the same.'

Berkeley accordingly adopted, and thenceforth until the sealing of the charter of 1676 there was used (both by him and by Herbert Jeffries, the Lieutenant Governor who relieved Berkeley after Bacon's Rebellion) a new form[38] as follows:

[Berkeley's form after the instructions of 1662]

To all to Whome these Presents Shall Come.
I, Sr. William Berkeley Kn^t, Govr & Capt Gen^{ll} of Virgin^a, send Greeting In O^t Lord God Everlasting.
Whereas by instrucons from the Kings Most Excellent Ma^{ty} directed to me & the Councell of State His Ma^{ty} was gratiously pleased to Authorize me the sayd Govr and the Councell to grant pattents and to assigne such portions of Land to all Adventurers and planters as have bin usuall heretofore in the Like Cases, Either for Adventures of money or Transportation of people into this Colony, according to a Charter of Orders from the Late Treasurer & Company and that the same portion of Fifty acres of Land be granted & Assigned for every

person transported hither since Midsummer of 1625 and that the same Course be continued to all Adventurers and planters untill it shall be otherwise determined By his Maᵗʸ.

Now Know Yee that I the sayd Sʳ William Berkeley Kⁿᵗ &c did with the consent of the Counsell of state &c accordingly give & grant unto . . . acres of land situate lyeing & being in . . . County, Bounded, vidzt . . .

To Have & to Hold the sayd Land with his due share of all mines & minneralls therein Conteyned, with all Rights and priveleges of Hunting Hawking fishing & fowling, with all Creeks Waters & Rivers, with all proffitts Comodyties & hereditments Whatsoever belonging to the sayd Land, to him the sayd . . . his Heirs & Assigns for Ever, in as large & Ample manner to all intents & purposes as is Expressed in a Charter of Orders from the Late Treasurer & Company dated the 18th day of November, 1618, or by Consequence may be justly collected out of the same or out of the Letters pattent whereon they are Grounded; To be held of oʳ Sovereyn Lord the King, his heirs & Successors for Ever, as of his mannoᵘʳ of East Greenwich, in free & comon soccage & not in Capite nor by Knᵗˢ service;

Yeilding & payeing to oʳ sayd Sovereigne Lord the King his Heirs & Successors for every fifty acres of land herein by these presents given and graunted, yearly att the feast of St. Michael the Archangell [September 29], the ffee Rent of one shilling to his Majestys use; which payment is to be made yearly from yeare to yeare, according to his Maᵗʸᵉˢ instructions of the 12ᵗʰ of 7ber 1662

Provided that if the Sayd . . . his Heirs or Assignes doe not Seate or plant or Cause to be planted or Seated on the sayd Land within three years Next Ensueing, then it shall be lawful for any Adventurer or planter to make Choyse or Seate thereupon.

Given att James Citty under my hand and Seale of the Colony this . . . day of . . . And in the . . . year of the Reign of our Sovereigne Lord King Charles the Second &c.

As this new patent form introduced nothing unprecedented except a regulation of revenues, which from the beginning had been reserved in principle both to the Company and to the Crown as its successor, it was accepted without question by the planters. Berkeley seems, however, to have gone further a few years later and asserted that the royal prerogative vested in the Governor a discretion in allowing individual grants. This was a direct challenge to the franchise itself and immediately precipitated a protest. The record of the incident is

obscure and may be interpreted only in the light of subsequent
events. A brief resolution of the Assembly in June, 1666,[39]
shows that it had been then argued in opposition to the Governor's claims that as, under the *Orders and Constitutions,* the
granting of lands was a function of the delegated self-government such grants might be made by the Assembly itself. The
judgment of the House was, however, that 'grants of land do
appertain only to the governor and council.' This was undoubtedly a sound interpretation of the colonial constitution,
but the discussion was important for it served as another bul-
wark of the 'commonwealth' principle; henceforth it was recognised in practice that the Governor had no more power over
land grants than that secured by his individual vote in the
Council.

Perhaps it was this incident which suggested to the Assembly in 1675 that it was expedient to stipulate for another
royal recognition of the head right. In their argument[40] for a
charter of 'incorporation' to enable Virginia to buy out those
Arlington and Northern Neck charters which had realized the
predictions made at the time of Lord Baltimore's charter, the
Virginia agents, Francis Moryson, Thomas Ludwell and Robert Smith represented:

'and since by experience tis found that the quantity fifty
acres for every person hath next to the blessing of God (and
the indulgent care of our most gracious princes) been the
greatest means of promoting the settlement of that country
and bringing it to the present hopeful condition that now it is
in, and from whence arises so great an emolument to the
Crown and Kingdom: we therefore humbly pray that the same
encouragement may be continued (as before used) to all adventurers thither.'

The occurrence of Bacon's Rebellion, after the charter so
solicited had been authorized but was still on its passage
through the seals, dashed the hopes of the colony in respect to
it, but in the matter of the head right the modified charter
actually sealed under date of October 10, 1676,[41] was duly
specific in a provision,

'That for the incouragement of such our subjects as shall from time to time go to dwell in the said plantation there shall be assigned out of the lands not already appropriated to every person so comeing to dwell, fifty acres of land, according as hath been used and allowed since the first plantation, to be held of us, our heirs and successors, as of our manor of East Greenwich, in our county of Kent, in free and common soccage.'

In pursuance of this charter, Secretary Thomas Ludwell thereafter proposed, and was duly authorized by the Assembly[42] to use, a new form of patent set out in the statute as follows:

[Ludwell's form, under the charter of 1676]

'*To all to whom &c. I &c. send &c.*

'*Whereas* his most sacred majestie hath been gratiously pleased by his royall letters pattents under the greate seal of England bearing date at Westminster the tenth day of October in the twenty-eight yeare of his raigne, among other things, in his said letters pattents, to continue and confirme the antient privileges and power of granting ffifty acres of land for every person imported into this his majesties colony of Virginia.

'*Now Know Yee* that I the said &c. doe with the consent of the council of State give and grant unto A. B. &c.'

This form was used by Culpeper and by all the successive Governors and Presidents to and including Nott and Jenings. It was Spotswood who inaugurated the last and most familiar patent form, that which was used thenceforth by all his successors, to and including Lord Dunmore. The circumstances of the adoption of this instrument open the last chapter of the history of the colonial land law in Virginia.

Bacon's Rebellion marks the end of an era of Virginia's territorial expansion. During the generation between 1646 and 1676 the colony pushed north across the indian boundary established by Berkeley's treaty with Necotowance and, passing both York and Rappahannock rivers, reached up the Potomac. In this process there was introduced the practice of speculation

in frontier lands as distinguished from actual seating of plantations.   Down to the end of the seventeenth century the
individual possession of a thousand acres was unusual in the
lower tidewater, but the earliest land grants on the Potomac
include a number of three and four times that area.   That
these were purely speculative holdings is evident from the fact
that no real effort was made to populate them.   When title
was perfected at all it was by compliance with what Spotswood
later called 'a sham condition of seating and planting.'   As a
consequence the indians continued to range these dividends
freely, and there were frequent contacts between them and the
few tenants who were sent to take post on the new frontier.
It was such an incident that brewed the storm on which Bacon
rode to his destruction.

The indian treaty of 1677 for the first time confined the
tributaries to surveyed and duly limited reservations.[43]   This
opened new opportunities for speculation by the tidewater
planters, in Pamunkey Neck (which ultimately became King
William and Hanover) and on the South Side beyond the
Blackwater River, in that part of Charles City which became
Prince George.   The planting of these territories is of prime
importance in the present study, for it had the unexpected
consequence of effecting a fundamental change in the basis
of seating waste lands.

The earliest entries in the Pamunkey Neck and Blackwater swamp were so liberal in the measure of individual
claims as to challenge the attention of the English government,
and in 1690 an Order in Council suspended further surveys.
The Assembly was prompt to protest, and, after an elaborate
investigation and adjudication of the merits of the outstanding
surveys, the restraint was removed and seating was resumed.[44]
Something of a scramble then ensued.   Edmund Jenings lead
off in his own interest and James Blair followed in the interest of William and Mary College.   He had inserted in the
charter of that institution a provision that 10,000 acres on
each of the new frontiers should be set aside for the support
of education.[45]   When the Commissary located the college

lands in Pamunkey Neck he conflicted with surveys which Secretary Ralph Wormeley had there made, on individual entries, for the hitherto unprecedented area of 13,000 acres in one parcel. Mutual caveats were filed and the ensuing controversy brought to light not only the methods followed by the land speculators but the degradation to which they had submitted the ancient franchise of the head right.

Considering the Commissary's interest, it can hardly have been by accident that the Hartwell, Chilton and Blair tract of 1697[46] took occasion to animadvert upon Virginia's land laws and, incidentally, to point out that, to the serious injury of the colony, head rights had become a colonial currency. Here is the searching criticism of that state paper, which accomplished a fundamental change in Virginia's land law:

'The method settled by the King in the first seating of the country was to allot 50 acres of land to everyone who should adventure within the country. Had this been observed it had been a lasting encouragement to adventurers to come, until the whole country was peopled. But as matters have been managed, the land has gone from the King and the country is very ill peopled.

'The first great abuse of this design arose from the ignorance and knavery of surveyors, who often gave out drafts of surveys without ever coming on the land. They gave their descriptions by some natural bounds and were sure to allow large measure, so that the persons for whom they surveyed should enjoy much larger tracts than they paid quit rents for.

'Then all Courts were very lavish in allowing certificates for rights: for if a master of a ship came into any Court and swore that he had imported himself and so many seamen and passengers at divers times into the country, and that he never elsewhere made use of these rights, he presently obtained an order for so many rights (i. e., so many times 50 acres of land) and these rights he would sell for a small matter. Perhaps the same seamen at another Court swore that they had adventured themselves so many times into the country and had not obtained an order for so many rights.

'Likewise the masters who bought the servants thus imported would at another Court make oath that they had bought so many persons who had adventured themselves into the country and obtained so many rights. Thus the land still went away and the adventurers who remained in the country had the least share of it.

'Again great liberties were used in issuing certificates for rights by the County Clerks, and especially by those of the Secretary's office, which was, and still is, a constant mint of those rights, where they may be purchased at from one shilling to five shillings per right.[47]

'The Government connived at these things, thinking it a very pardonable crime that the King's land should be given away to people who had no right to it, since in this way the land was taken up and the King had so much more quit rent paid to him, whereas land not taken up paid nothing.

'But they did not consider that the small profit of quit rents does not balance the great damage of leaving the country without inhabitants, which is the result of their method: for the King and Kingdom of England gain near two hundred times as much by one ordinary planter as the King would have got by the quit rent of the 50 acres which he should have had.

'This may be worked out thus. A usual crop of tobacco for one head is 2,000 lbs., which, at 6d. per lb. (the present duty in England), amounts to £50. Suppose this 2,000 lbs. of tobacco to be put into three hogsheads and here is 6s. of Virginia duty to the King, by the two shillings per hogshead duty. Then the freight of this at £8 per ton comes to £6, which is commonly paid in England, making in all £56, 6s., od. besides the increase of ships and seamen and the multitudes maintained by the manufacture of tobacco in England and of English goods sold the planters.

'To find out on the other hand how many acres it will require to make £56, 6s., od. out of quit rents: quit rent tobacco is sold *communibus annis* at 5s. per hundred, and taking 24 lbs. of tobacco as rent for every hundred acres,[48] at that rate £56, 6s., od. will purchase 22,520 lbs. of tobacco, which is the quit rent of 93,833 acres of land.

'Hence one man's labour is equivalent to the quit rents of near a hundred thousand acres of land, which was the quantity allotted for two thousand men. Moreover, the quit rents would not have been lost but would have been paid at last, when the country came to be peopled.

'This fundamental error of letting the King's land run away to lie waste, together with another of not seating in townships, is the cause that Virginia today is so ill peopled.

'Everyone who takes out a patent for any tract of the King's land is by the patent obliged to two things, viz: to seat or plant upon it within three years, otherwise it lapses to the King; and to pay quit rent of one shilling for every fifty acres per annum. Seating is reckoned the building of a house and keeping a stock one whole year: it matters not how small the house is, a hog house serves the turn. Planting the law reckons to be the planting and tending one acre of ground no matter how badly. Either of these within three years of the date of the patent saves the whole tract, be it ever so large; and this is the cause that though all the good land in the country is taken up, there is very little improvement on it.[49]

'Land which is neither seated nor planted after three years lapses to the King, and is called lapsed land: but it never comes into the King's hand, being due by local law to the first who petitions the General Court for it.'

Impressed by this constructive criticism, the Lords of Trade inserted in Nicholson's instructions of 1698 a direction that the Governor should propose to the Assembly a new system of land grants, founded on settlement rather than importation rights. They argued that

'any person having 100 negroes may take up 19,000 acres of land, which is more than can be cultivated by one owner, and so in proportion for any greater or lesser number: by which means all the lands remaining ungranted in the colony may fall into a few rich men's hands, which will be a discouragement to such persons as might go to settle there.'

As Nicholson was unable to get any support for this proposal in the Assembly, the Lords of Trade followed with a definite instruction for Governor Nott in 1705, intended, by abolition of the head right, to prevent the holding of lands in the dead hand. The Council then raised the constitutional point that this violated the charter of 1676, and the offending instruction was necessarily withdrawn.[50] Meanwhile the Assembly had realized the expediency of itself putting an end to the traffic in head rights. They sought to do this, however, without jeopardy to land speculation, which no one in the colony had any intention to forego; to that end they now relied on the new 'treasury right,' which, as will appear, had been invented in 1699. In respect to the

head right, the Committee, which was formulating the Revisal
of 1705, devised the following provision:

'That all and every person, male or female, imported and
coming into this colony and dominion free, has a right to fifty
acres of land; and every Christian servant, male or female,
imported, after he or she becomes free or time of service is
expired, has a right to fifty acres of land for his or her importation; and every person coming into this colony and importing a wife, or children under age, hath a right to fifty
acres of land for himself, his wife and every such child so
imported; and certificate thereof shall be granted to every
such free person and master of a family demanding the same,
and to every servant after such their freedom in manner and
form as is by this act hereafter directed; and that no person
or persons by virtue of such importations shall hereafter claim
any right to land other than the persons so imported as aforesaid, or those to whom they shall assign their right in the
presence of two witnesses; any law, usage or custom to the
contrary in any wise notwithstanding.
'*Provided always* That nothing herein contained shall be
construed to give a right to any factor, master of a ship, or
other seafaring man not settling him or themselves, and be-
coming tithable in the country, to claim or take up any land
by colour of his or their importation, nor to any person whatsoever to claim a right for his importation more than once.'

This legislation introduced self-imposed restraints which
regulated some of the seventeenth century abuses.   Thenceforth the head right was to be the peculiar right of a free man
who became a tithable.   Thus were excluded not only the
claims of ship master, merchant and planter in respect to the
importation of white servants, but also all claims founded on
negro slaves.   More than that, the act of 1705 prohibited the
practice of counting as a head right more than one arrival of
the same individual.

But despite these constructive provisions (as well as others
which, as Benjamin Watkins Leigh was to say, made the act
of 1705 'the basis of all our subsequent land laws'), when
the Lords of Trade read what the Assembly proposed, they
concluded, not without reason, that it did not meet Hartwell's

criticism by inhibiting speculative land holding, and the act was disallowed.[51]

As it fell out, this veto served only to complicate the situation. When Spotswood reached Virginia one of his first reports was that,

'Since the repeal of that act people have begun to practice the same fraudulent way of proving rights for importation."

The Governor himself took hold of the problem vigorously. Without warrant of law, but relying upon the tenor of his instructions, he invoked the prerogative and made the constructive features of the act of 1705 effective by proclamation. In doing so he introduced a new form of head right patent which followed closely the precedent proposed by the Assembly. To bring home to the people his thesis that it was Queen Anne's land they were taking up and not their own, he conformed the patents to the writs issuing from the law courts and substituted the name of the Soveign as grantor, in place of that of the Governor; and in lieu of the traditional recitals of the Orders and Constitutions of 1618 and of the Charter of 1676 he substituted a general rehearsal of 'divers good causes and consideracons.' This obscured the franchise but, of course, did not destroy it. Moreover, he restored the Crown's 'royalty' in mines, which the act of 1705 had ignored; he introduced a provision for forfeiture in case of three years' default in payment of quit rents; and, finally, he tightened up the conditions of seating.

This final testimony for the head right franchise was accordingly as follows:[52]

[Spotswood's head right form]

Anne, by the Grace of God of Great Britain, France and Ireland, Queen Defender of the Faith &c.

To all to whom these presents shall come, Greeting.

Know Ye that for divers good causes and consideracons, but more especially for and in consideration of the importation of one person to dwell within this our colony of Virginia, whose name is William Shorman,

We have given, granted and confirmed, and by these presents for us, our heirs and successors, do give, grant and confirm unto John Wade of the county of James Citty one certain tract or parcell of land in same containing 47 acres, and bounded as followeth, to-wit: . . .

With all woods, underwoods, Swamps, Marshes, Lowgrounds, Meadows, Feedings, and his due share of all Veins, Mines and Quarries as well discovered as not discovered within the bounds aforesaid, same being part of the said quantity of 47 acres of land, and also the Rivers, Waters and Water Courses therein contained, together with the Privileges of Hunting, Hawking, Fishing, Fowling, and all other Profits, commodities and Hereditaments whatsoever to the same or any part thereof belonging or in any wise appertaining.

To Have, Hold, Possess and enjoy the said Tract or Parcell of Land and all other the before mentioned and granted Premises and every part thereof, with their and every of their appurtenances unto the said John Wade and to his heirs and assigns forever, To the only use and behoof of him the said John Wade, his heirs and assigns forever.

To be held of us, our Heirs and successors as of our Manor of East Greenwich in the county of Kent, in free and common soccage and not in capite or by Knight's service.

Yielding and paying unto us, our heirs and successors for every fifty acres of Land (and so proportionably for a lesser or greater Quantity than fifty acres) the Fee Rent of one Shilling yearly, to be paid upon the Feast of Saint Michael the Archangel [September 29].

And also cultivating and improving three acres part of every fifty of the Tract above mentioned within three years after the date of these Presents.

Provided always that if three years of the said Fee Rent shall at any time be in arrear and unpaid, or if the said John Wade, his heirs or assigns do not within the space of three years next coming after the date of these Presents, cultivate and improve three acres part of every fifty of the Tract above mentioned, then the estate hereby granted shall cease and be utterly determined; and thereafter it shall and may be lawful to and for us, our heirs and Successors to grant the same lands and premises with the appurtenances unto such other Person or Persons as we, our heirs and Successors shall think fit.

In Witness Whereof we have caused these our Letters Patent to be made.

Witness our Trusty and well beloved Alexander Spotswood, Esquire, our Lieut. Governor and Commander in Chief of our said Colony and Dominion at Williamsburgh, under the seal of our said colony the 12th day of December, one thousand seven hundred and ten, in the ninth year of our Reign.

Spotswood's legally questionable proceedings were acquiesced in partly because they were economically sound, partly because they were in line with what the Assembly had proposed, but chiefly because they did not interfere with the speculators. As they had opportunity (*e. g.*, when Spotsylvania and Brunswick were organized) those gentry went on to 'enter for' larger tracts of frontier land than ever before, and sometimes to hold them undeveloped for many years.

It is interesting that after Spotswood had retired from the government he too became a frontier landholder. Indeed, the 85,000 acres he put together in one boundary before 1727, reaching eight or ten miles about Germanna, made him the tallest tree in that forest until Robert Carter outgrew him.[53] In doing this he did not, however, belie his earlier denunciation of the speculators. Uniformly, he had directed his criticism not to the extent of the holdings, but to the dog in the manger policy by which the 'great tracts' remained 'for the greatest part uncultivated to the great prejudice of the colony and the discouragement of future adventurers where they can find little or no convenient land to plant upon.'[54] Spotswood made sincere and expensive efforts more than technically to 'plant' his lands and at last secured confirmation of his patents because, after long delay and careful investigation, the Privy Council found that he had employed his entries 'more than any other Person towards peopling the country.' In this, then, he set an example which some, if not all, the speculators followed, and so justified the support of 'manors'[55] as institutions by two of the ablest of Spotswood's successors as Governor.

In 1728 Gooch reported:[56]

'I am credibly informed that without taking up those large tracts upon which great improvements were necessary to be made those counties [Spotsylvania and Brunswick] would not have been settled so speedily as they have been, and much of that land which has been seated in small parcells would in all probability have remained to this day desolate; as may be seen in the County of Brunswick, which having but few great tracts of land taken up in it by Men of Substance, hath advanced very little in the number of its inhabitants in proportion to the other county, Spotsilvania, where the greatest tracts have been granted and possessed, and thereby given encouragement to the meaner sort of people to seat themselves, as it were, under the shade and protection of the Greater.'

In 1754 Dinwiddie endorsed this with a certificate that:[57]

'The granting of large quantities to one Person has been of service in settling the back and remote parts of this Dominion, as these great grants have been subdivided to poor people that come from the other colonies and are not able to be at the charge of coming here [i. e., to Williamsburg] and taking out Grants for small quantities of land.'

By the middle of the eighteenth century the practice of 'manors,' in the ancient sense of that word, connoting an entailed parcel of land cultivated on lease by a number of customary tenants, had thus taken a recognised, if never an altogether successful, place in the westward movement of the Virginia people. Considering, however, the fundamental objections to the practice, it was happily no longer founded on a misuse of the head right. The rights used to create the 'manors' were unformly 'treasury rights.'

In this competition the head right itself withered and fell into desuetude. Before 1715, it had ceased to have any practical importance as a factor in building Virginia civilization.[58]

§ 2.   *The Treasury Right*

When Michael Drayton composed, in the summer of 1606, his fine ode, *To the Virginian Voyage,* as an incentive to participation in the expedition which sailed a few months later to establish 'the First Colony in Virginia,' and therein included the stanza:

> *And cheerefully at Sea*
> *Successe you still intice*
> *To get the pearle and gold,*
> *And ours to hold*
> *Virginia*
> *Earth's only Paradise,*

he summed up not only the political and commercial aspirations of the Virginia Company, but the very terms of what we would now call the stock certificate it was then issuing to subscribers. This will appear by comparison of the poet with a 'bill of adventure' which has survived, as follows:

'*Whereas* Henry Dawkes now bound on the intended voyage to Virginia hath paid, in ready mony, to Sr. Thomas Smith Kt. Treasurer for Virginia the some of twelve pounds tenn shillings for his Adventure in the Voyage to Virginia,
'*It is agreed* that for the same the said Henry Dawkes his heires, Executors, Admrs. and assignes shall have rateably according to his Adventure his full pte. of all such lands tenemts. and hereditamts. as shall from time to time bee there planted and inhabited, And of all such Mines and Minneralls of Gould, Silver and other mettalls or Treasures, pearles, pretious stoanes or any kinds of Wares or Merchandize, comodities or pfitts. whatsoever, which shal bee obtained or gotten in the said Voyage, According to the portion of money by him imployed to that Use, In as large and ample manner as any other Adventurer therein shall receave for the like some.
'*Written* this fowerteenth of July one Thousand six hundred and Eight.

Richard Atkinson.
[Clerk of the Virginia Company].'

The general dividend due to the holders of such bills of adventure was defined by the *Orders and Constitutions* of 1618 as follows:

'That all grants of Land in Virginia to such Adventurers as have heretofore brought in their money [i. e., the assessment of 1616] here to the Treasurer for their several shares (being Twelve Pound ten shillings the share) be of one hundred acres the share upon the first Division and of as many more upon a Second Division when the Land of the first Division shall be sufficiently peopled. And for every person which they shall transport thither within seven years after midsummer day 1618, if he continue there three years or die in the meantime after he is shipped, it be fifty acres the person upon the first division and fifty more upon a second division (the first being sufficiently peopled) without paying any rent to the Company for the one or the other.'

A typical and significant patent in pursuance of this franchise is that issued in September, 1632, to William Dawkes. His grant has the interest of being founded on rights accrued to the grantee's father, partly on the bill of adventure already quoted and partly on the head right of an ancient planter. It shows, too, that Henry Dawkes died in the colony and there left, to claim his dividend, a son who probably was born in the colony, as he claimed no head right in behalf of his own importation. This patent is further notable as showing the special privileges afforded to an ancient planter, not only in the double rate of dividend but in an immunity of that right from forfeiture for lack of seating. In that last respect, as is here recited, the ancient planter might be ousted of a patented boundary if he failed to seat it, but, unlike the newcomer, preserved the privilege of seating his dividend elsewhere until it was vested.

The patent follows:[59]

[A patent for an ancient planters treasury right]

By the Governr. and Capt. Generll. of Virginia:
To all to whome these prsents. shall come, I Sr. John Harvey Kt. Governr. and Capt. Generll. of Virginia send greeting in our Lord God Everlasting
Whereas by the orders and Constitutions made and sett forth by the late Company for the affaires of this Colony, It is ordered and appointed that all such lands and devidents as shall bee due to any Adventurers or planters within this Colony of what Condition soever they bee should bee laid out and assigned unto them by the Governr. and Councell here established
And whereas the same power and authoritie is graunted by his Majties Letters Pattents directed to mee and the Councell of State bearing date the six and twentieth day of March in the third yeare of his Majties Raigne that now is one Thousand six hundred twentie seaven
Now Know Yee that I the said Sr. John Harvey doe by the prsents. with the consent of the Councell of State give and grant unto William Dawkes of Verinas wthin the Corporacon of Charles Citty, planter, sonn and heire apparent of Henry Dawkes deceased and to his heires and assignes for ever
Twoe hundred acres of land as his land as his first devident and Upon a second division to bee augmented and doubled to him his said

heires and assignes when hee or they shall sufficiently have peopled and planted the same

Scituate and being wthin the Corporation of Charles Citty aforesaid abutting . . .

One hundred acres of the said land accrewing due unto him as being the lawfull heire of the said Henry Dawkes being an Ancient planter for his psonall devident and the other hundred due by a bill of Adventures of twelve pounds tenn shillings in the right of the said Henry Dawkes his father deceased, dated the fowerteenth day of July one Thousand six hundred and Eight and graunted unto him by an order of Court made the seaventh day of October last past

To have and to hold the said Twoe hundred acres of land wth the Apptennces wth his due share of all Mines and Minneralls therein conteyned, And wth all rights and priviledges of hunting, fishing, fowling and others wth in the princts. and upon the borders of the same, To the sole and pper. Use, benifitt and behoofe of him the said William Dawkes, his heires and assignes for ever

In as large and ample manner to all intents and purposes as is expressed in the said orders and Constitutions or by consequence may bee justly Collected out of the same or out of his Majties Letters Pattents whereon they are grounded

Yeilding and paying for every fiftie acres of Land herein by these prsents. given and graunted yearely at the feast of St. Michaell the Archangell [September 29] the fee rent of one shilling of lawfull mony of England.

Provided allwayes that if the said William Dawkes, his heires or assignes doe not seate or plant upon the said twoe hundred acres of land wthin the time and terme of three yeares now next ensuing the date hereof, That then it shall and may bee lawfull for any Adventurer or planter to make Choice and seate upon the same, And hee the said William Dawkes shall take up this devident in some other place.

In Witness Whereof I have here unto sett my hand and the seale of the Colony. *Given* at James Citty the seaventh day of September in the eighth yeare of the raigne of our Soveraigne Lord Charles by the grace of God of England, Scotland, France and Ireland, King, defender of the faith &c. and in the yeare of our Lord one Thousand six hundred thirtie twoe and in the XXVIth yeare of this Plantacon.

The Dawkes patent is the more significant because the early Patent Books record comparatively few grants founded like it on the treasury right. The explanation of this lack is found in a characteristic development of individualism among some of the London merchants who were enrolled among the Company's adventurers. Moved by a thoroughly English impatience of communistic conditions, these men began to strike out for themselves as soon as the Company had agreed, in 1616, to break up the 'common stock' and declare dividends of land to its members. They went so far, indeed, as to introduce the ferment of decay into the Company itself.[60]

What happened was that groups of adventurers began to pool their dividends and so secured grants in common of large contiguous areas of land on which they undertook to set up sub colonies of their own. To that end they enlisted emigrants, invested in supplies and sent out ships, all independently of the Company. Thus came into existence those 'particular plantations' which remain a challenge to the illumination of the historian. The evidence for them survives chiefly by reason of the fact that the management of the Company, clairvoyant to the disintegrating effect of separate cantons, sought in the *Orders and Constitutions* of 1618, to regulate them in detail. That they were by no means all alike either in constitution or size appears in the description of those which were being set up when Sir George Yeardley became Governor:

'And touching all other particular plantations set out or like to be set out in convenient multitudes either by divers of the ancient adventurers associating themselves together (as the Society of Smith's [afterwards Southampton] Hundred and Martin's Hundred) or by some ancient adventurer or Planter associating others unto him (as the plantation of Captain Samuel Argall, and Captain John Martin, and that by the late Lord Lamar advanced), or by some new adventurers joining themselves under one head (as the plantation of Christopher Lawes, gentleman, and others now in providing).'

We know further that upon these precedents, and perhaps in other forms, 'particular plantations' were diligently multiplied in the exercise of the treasury right until, between 1619, when the foregoing statement was made, and the dissolution in 1624, the Company had sealed on that account seventy-two additional large grants of land.[61]

It seems to have been intended that all of these cantons should have individual municipal status and the right of self-government in local affairs. The Company provided generally that, like the four principal Boroughs which it was itself planting (James Town, Charles City, Henrico and Kiccotan), the particular plantations should be 'bodies corporate,' wherefore provision was made for them, as for the Boroughs, to have grants of and to hold 'common lands' for the support of their magistrates.[62] But whatever was the intention, certainly they did not all have the same political development. Some were recognized as Hundreds and sent their own representatives to the early Assemblies to sit side by side, and to vote equally, with the representatives of the Boroughs, but others were denied that privilege. It is probable that the Assembly itself formulated and applied some standard of population as a condition of the promotion of a particular plantation into a Hundred, but the evidence of what that standard was is wanting.

Even the record of the location of all the particular plantations is meagre. The practice of the Company was to preserve, in that muniment chest which disappeared at the time of the dissolution, a 'counterpane' of every patent sealed in England, but apparently no detailed public record of them was set up in the colony, at least no such record has survived. We are thus remitted for the evidences of title in respect of the several Hundreds to such repatents as were made after the dissolution, upon a transfer from an original Society. The following patent of 1636, relating to Berkeley Hundred, must serve as an illustrative example of this chapter of the treasury right, even though the record is severely abbreviated. Short as it is, it stands as a testimony to the antiquity of two of the best known land marks on James River, viz:[63]

[The patent for a 'particular plantation,' Berkeley Hundred]

To all to whome these prsents shall come, I Sr. John Harvey Kt. Governr. &c. send &c.

Whereas by Instructions from the Kings most Excellent Majtie directed to mee and the Councell here resident, bearing date the 22th of May in the twelfth yeare of his Majties Reigne, His Majtie was gratiously pleased for the better encouragemt. of all Adventurers and planters to authorize and Command us to give and assigne to all freemen such pporcons of Lands as were heretofore given and graunted Unto the planters being freemen of this Colony.

Now Know Yee that I the said Sr. John Harvey Kt. doe by these prsents wth the consent of the Councell of State accordingly give and graunt Unto William Tucker, Maurice Tompson, George Tompson, William Harris, Thomas Deacon, James Stone, Cornelius Loyd of London, Merchants, and Jerimiah Blackman of London, Marrinr., and their Associates and Company, Eight Thousand acres of land, scituate, lying and being in the County of Charles Citty, being a tract of land commonly called by the name of Bearckley hundred,

Bounding East upon the land of Capt. Thomas Paulett, begining at a small gutt that runneth into the woods at the west end of the Clift of Westover, and West upon Kimiges Creeke . . .

The said Eight Thousand acres of Land being due unto them the said William Tucker & others as aforesaid by Deed of Sale from the Adventurers and Company of Bearckley hundred Exemplified Under the great seale of England and bearing date the   day of

To have and to hold the said &c.

Dated the 9th of February, 1636.

Ut in aliis.

After the dissolution had automatically suspended the creation of treasury rights, and those which accrued under the Company had been satisfied, the practice of acquiring land in that way lay fallow; but the tradition was kept alive. So it was when the indian lands in the Pamunkey Neck and on the South Side below the Blackwater Swamp, were definitely opened for seating in 1699, the old principle was revived. How this came about is set out in the 'Account of the Manner of Taking up Land,' which President Edmund Jenings sent home in 1706,[64] viz:

'The Company at first settled the method of granting land two ways, To witt, Either for the importing of persons, or adventures of money into the Colony and thereupon 50 acres of Land was granted for every person imported, and 100 acres for every 12 li. 10s. adventured towards the plantation.

'Afterwards, about the year 1624, the Government of Virginia was taken from the Company and invested immediately in the Crown, but still the usual method of granting land for importacion was confirmed and continued and accordingly it was always practised by the Governor and Council to grant lands either for a man's own personal adventure or for such others as he had imported [or] for such Rights as he hath purchased of any other person. . . .

'And thus the method of granting Land continued without any alteration till the year 1699, and then several persons having Rights to Lands in Pamunkey Neck, and on the South Side of the Blackwater Swamp, who could not well procure legal Rights for patenting thereof, and the Treasury of the Country for support of the Government being very Low, a method was established for selling those Rights at a certain rate for money to be paid to the Auditor and Receiver of Revenues for the use of the Crown, To witt, that whosoever would pay the Auditor five shillings for the King's use should have the same right to take up and patent 50 acres of Land, that he might otherwise have had for the importacion of any person into this Colony. But the other method of granting lands for Importacion was never pretended to be taken away, but still continues.'

It will be observed that the new 'treasury right' was thus made the equivalent not of two but of one head right, and that its value was fixed at the maximum price current of the depreciated head right, as reported by Hartwell, Chilton and Blair, in 1697.

This action of the Council was duly ratified by the Assembly in the act of 1705, when provision was made for a special patent form to give it effect. The declaration of the act was as follows:

'That if any person not having right to any land for importation as aforesaid, shall be willing and desirous to take up and plant any land in this colony, it shall and may be lawful to and for every such person to obtain a right thereto, in manner following, that is to say: the person desiring such right shall pay unto her majesties receiver generall of the revenues in this dominion for the time being, for and towards the better support of the government of this her majesties colony and dominion and the contingent charges thereof, the Sum of five shillings current money for every fifty acres of land he or she intends to take up and plant . . .'

Although, as has been shown, that act was vetoed by the Crown and there was no further legislation in respect to the treasury right, the Council continued the practice without objection either from the Assembly or from the imperial government.   Indeed, everybody concerned, the land speculators and the local treasury, were pleased with it.   Spotswood testified to this in his annual report for 1717.

'The Revenue consists,' he said,[65] 'of . . . lastly, 5s. paid for his Majesty's use for the right of taking up 50 acres of his Majesty's land when the taker has not a right by Importation.   This was first established in the year 1699, when there was a greater demand for land than the Rights, allowed by the charter, for persons imported would answer; and has since proved a good Expedient to encrease the Revenue and to render the taking up of land more easy to the people.'

The treasury right patent, which was that under which were created most of the later eighteenth century land titles on the Virginia frontier, was accordingly in the following form. The formal clauses were identical with those of Spotswood's head right patent which has been quoted, viz:[66]

[The XVIII Century treasury right form]

George &c. To all &c.
Know Ye that for divers good causes and consideracons but more especially for and in consideracon of the Sum of Sixteen pounds five Shillings of good and lawfull money for our use paid to our Receiver General of our Revenues in this our Colony and Dominion of Virginia
We have given, granted and confirmed and by these presents for us, our heirs and Successors do give, grant and confirm unto William Robertson of the City of Williamsburgh one certain tract or parcell of Land containing three thousand two hundred and twenty-nine acres lying and being about twenty miles above the falls of Rapahannock river in the parish of St. George in the County of Essex and bounded as followeth, to witt, Beginning (on the South side the South river called Rappidanna) at . . .
With all &c. [verbatim as in Spotswood's head right form, *supra*]
  To have, hold &c.
  To be held &c.
  Yeilding & paying &c.
  Provided &c.
  In Witness &c.
Witness our Trusty and wellbeloved Alexander Spotswood our Lt. Governor &c., at Williamsburgh under the Seal of our Said Colony

the Last day of October one thousand seven hundred and Sixteen in
the third year of our Reign.

§ 3. *The Military Right*

When, in October 1630, Virginia faced the perilous domain of old Opechancanough across the estuary we now call
York River

> *Litora litoribus contraria, fluctibus undas*
> . . . *arma armis,*

the Council adopted a florid order, which laid down the policy
under which George Washington was ultimately to secure his
Kenawha lands.

As recited in a land patent of July 6, 1636,[67] this order
was as follows:

'*Whereas* the Usual policy and Custome of all Nations, but
in more espetiall manner of the State of England, have as well
in antient as Modern Times, for the safeguard and securitie
of the Inland Country, afforded and induced the Frontier Inhabitants with diverse privileges and immunities tending to the
inabling them to make the better resistance against both open
invasion and sudden incursions of the neare confining and Contiguous Enemie according to the rules of Justice and Equity,
poised thereby and ballancing their greater and more immanent
share of danger with the guerdon and reward of spetiall and
particular and fitt instic'on,

'*Wherefore* the Governor and Councell by order of Court
bearing date at James Citty the 8th of October, 1630, for the
securing and taking in of a tract of land called the forrest,
bordering upon the Cheife residence of the Pamunky King, the
most dangerous head of the Indian Enemie, did after much
consultation thereof decree and sett doune severall Portions of
land for each Commander and fifteen acres p. polle for all
other persons, who for the first year, and five and twenty acres
per poll for all such whoe the second yeare, should adventure
or be adventured to seate and inhabite on the Southern side of
Pamunkye river, now called Charles River and then Knowne
by the Indian name of Chiscake, as a reward and encouragement for such their undertaking, as by the said order more at
large appeareth.'

The principle here applied was that a special waiver of the constitutional methods of land acquisition was justifiable in the general welfare; specifically that the dedication of a portion of the 'common stock' of land in consideration of the establishment of a military barrier, which would inure to the protection of the community as a whole, was within that purview.

This precedent was persistently followed as the frontier widened. The next application of it was in 1646, when, following the peace with Necotowance, the Assembly decided to retrench the public expense of maintaining the four forts which Governor Berkeley had built against the Pamunkeys. Then it was resolved[68] that grants of the forts and some surrounding lands should be made to the captains who had commanded those outposts in consideration of their continuing to garrison them for three years at their own expense. In pursuance of this new recognition of the military right, patents were accordingly issued, after the condition had been complied with: on March 14, 1649/50, to Roger Marshall, for Fort Royal (alias Rickahock) at Pamunkey, with 600 acres; on June 9, 1653, to Abraham Wood, for Fort Henry at the falls of Appomattox River, with 600 acres; and on August 8, 1653, to Thomas Rolfe, for Fort James on the Chickahominy Ridge, with 400 acres.[69]

The recital of the consideration for these grants was, e. g.,

'*Whereas* by Act of the Assembly dated at James Cittie the 5th day of October, 1646, Fort Royal als. Ricahock, with Six hundred acres of Land joyning upon the same with all Houses and Edifices belonging to the same was graunted unto Capt. Roger Marshall upon condicon that he the said Capt. Marshall should Maynetayne ten Men upon the same during the time of three years, which said Condicon being performed,
'*Now Know Yee* that I the said Sr. William Berkeley, &c., accordingly doe give and graunt, &c.'

On the same principle was formulated the act of September 29, 1701,[70] 'for the better strengthening the frontiers and discovering the approaches of an enemy,' which provided for land grants equivalent to quadruple the head right to those who would undertake the defense of the frontier under the discipline of a 'Society,' viz:

'There shall be granted to every certain number of men who shall enter into society and agree to undertake such cohabitation any quantity of land not under the quantity of 10,000 acres nor exceeding the quantity of 30,000 acres upon any of the frontiers within this government wherever it shall be found not legally taken up or possessed by any of his majesty's leige people, which land shall be held by such societys or companes of men in common as tenants in common and undivided to them and each of them . . . forever . . .

'*Provided always* and it is the true intent and meaning of this act that for every five hundred acres of land to be granted in pursuance of this act there shall be and shall continually be kept upon the said land one Christian warlike man between sixteen and sixty years of age, perfect of limbs, able and fitt for service, who shall also be continually provided with a well fixed musquet or fuzee, a good pistoll, sharp simeter, tomahawk and five pounds of good clean pistoll powder and twenty pounds of sizable leaden bulletts or swann or goose shott, to be kept within the fort directed by this act, besides the powder and shott for his necessary or usefull shooting at game.'

It does not appear that any company of the 'warlike Christian men' described in this act ever took advantage of it; certainly the Patent Books show no grant under it. The explanation is doubtless found in the individualism of the Virginian. The kind of men the Assembly wanted to plant on the frontier were the 'long knives' who preferred each one to shift for himself and not be bound to the discipline of any 'Society.' The theory of the act of 1701 was, however, contemporaneously applied in the allotment of 10,000 acres at Manakintown, above the falls of James River, to the French Huguenot refugees who were then pouring into Virginia.[71] Still later that same motive actuated the unfulfilled promise in 1709 of a land grant on the upper Potomac to Christopher de Graffenried;[72] as it did the exemptions and other privileges offered all settlers on the frontier by the Spotsylvania and Brunswick act of 1720.[73] It was applied again in the Orders

in Council relating to the Van Meter (Hite) lands on the
Shenandoah in 1730;[74] as it was in those later orders voted
by the Council to several of their own members, e. g., Thomas
Lee's Ohio Company and John Lewis' Loyal Company, both
in 1749; as well as Speaker John Robinson's Greenbrier Company in 1751.[75]

The most conspicuous applications of the military right
to land grants were, however, the two which arose out of the
French and Indian War. In the first this took the form of an
offer of frontier land to induce voluntary military service, and
in the second of a bounty or reward for such service already
performed; but back of both offers was the ulterior expectation of the government that the warrior would remain on
the frontier and so serve as a military barrier for the future.

Robert Dinwiddie has been given the credit of inaugurat-
ing this last practice, but the form the action took shows that
it was strictly in the Virginia tradition we have cited. The
Governor's demand upon the Assembly for funds with which
to wage war upon the French, following Washington's capitulation at Great Meadows, resulted in the act of February, 1754,
'for the encouragement and protection of settlers upon the
Waters of the Mississippi.'[76] By this legislation there was
authorized a loan of £10,000 on the faith of certain special
taxes, the proceeds to be administered for 'protecting and defending his majesty's subjects who are now settled or hereafter shall settle on the waters of the river Mississippi.' Dinwiddie's organization was to give effect to this act. His dispatch to Lord Holderness of March 12, 1754,[77] retails what
he did:

'My Lord, the Bounds of the Proprietary Govts. of Maryland and Pennsylvania are limited to the Westward. That of
P., I think, is five degrees west of the easternmost part of their
present Settlements. Maryland is not so extensive. The Lands
to the West of these boundaries I conceive to be properly in his
Majesty's Dominion of Virginia, which will make it very extensive. After our Assembly were prevailed on to vote £10,000
I thought it necessary, to give Encouragement to the People
to enlist with Spirit, to grant them 200,000 acres of his Maj-

esty's Lands on the Ohio, 15 years without paying Quit rents. Copy of the Proclamation I enclose you. The reason I went on was to engage the People that went on the Expedition to remain there and make Settlements, and I think it better to give that Quantity to our People than to acquit Possession to the French of as many Millions of Acres, and I therefore hope it will meet with His Majesty's royal approbation.'

The Governor's proclamation, so described, was issued under date of February 19, 1754.[78] After reciting his determination to build a fort on the Ohio at the fork of the Monongahela, to check the encroachments of the French, he proceeded:

'For an encouragement to all who shall voluntarily enter into the said service, I do hereby notify and promise, by and with the advice and consent of his Majesty's Council of this Colony, that over and above their pay 200,000 acres of His Majesty, the King of Great Britain's Lands on the east side of the River Ohio, within this Dominion (100,000 acres to be contiguous to the said Fort and the other 100,000 acres to be on or near the River Ohio) shall be laid off and granted to such persons who by their voluntary engagement and good behavior in the said service shall deserve the same; and I further promise that the said lands shall be divided amongst them immediately after the performance of the said service in a proportion due to their respective merit.'

Dinwiddie provided further that all lands so granted might be held free of quit rents for 15 years, but, unfortunately for those who accepted his offer, the home government thought that in this respect the Governor had been too liberal.

An important chapter in the life of George Washington is that of his efforts to secure for himself, and the officers who served under him in the campaign of 1754, the fruits of this proclamation. That he did so at last, after nearly twenty years of waiting, appears in a series of patents issued by Lord Dunmore in 1772, of which the following is an example:[79]

[Dunmore's patents in pursuance of Dinwiddie's proclamation of 1753]

George the Third by the Grace of God of Great Britain, France and Ireland, King Defender of the Faith &c.

To All to Whom these Presents shall come—Greeting.

Know Ye that for divers good Causes and Considerations but more Especially for the Consideration mentioned in a Proclamation of Robert Dinwiddie Esquire late Lieutenant Governor and Commander in Chief of our Colony and Dominion of Virginia bearing date the Nineteenth day of February One Thousand seven Hundred and Fifty four, For encouraging Men to Enlist in the Service of our late Royal Grandfather for the Defence and Security of the said Colony

We Have Given, Granted & Confirmed and by these Presents for us, our Heirs and Successors Do Give, Grant and Confirm unto George Washington Esquire one Certain Tract or Parcel of Land Containing two Thousand four Hundred and forty eight Acres, lying and being in the County of Botetourt, and bounded as followeth, to-wit:

Beginning at or near the upper end of the fourth large Bottom on the East side of the Ohio, and about sixteen Miles below the little Konawa . . .

With all Woods, Underwoods, Swamps, Marshes, Lowgrounds, Meadows, Feedings & his due Share of all Veins, Mines & Quarries as well discovered as not discovered within the bounds aforesaid & being part of the said Quantity of two Thousand four Hundred & Forty eight Acres of Land & the Rivers, Waters & Water Courses therein contained, together with the Privileges of Hunting, Hawking, Fishing, Fowling & all other Profits Commodities & Hereditaments whatsoever to the same or any part thereof belonging or in any wise appertaining.

To Have, Hold, Possess & Enjoy the said Tract or Parcel of Land & all other the before granted Premises & every part thereof with their & every of their Appurtenances unto the said George Washington & to his Heirs & Assigns forever to the only use & Behoof of him the said George Washington, his Heirs & Assigns forever.

To be Held of us, our Heirs & Successors as of our Manor of East Greenwich in the County of Kent in free and Common Soccage & not in Capite or by Knights Service

Yielding and Paying unto us, our Heirs & Sucessors for every fifty Acres of Land & so proportionately for a lesser or greater Quantity than fifty Acres the fee Rent of one Shilling Yearly to be paid upon the Feast of Saint Michael the Arch Angel [September 29], next after fifteen Years from the date of these Presents & also Cultivating & Improving three acres part of every Fifty of the Tract above mentioned within three Years after the Date of these Presents.

Provided always that if three Years of the said Fee Rent from & after the expiration of the fifteen Years aforesaid shall at any time be in arrear & unpaid or if the said George Washington, his

Heirs or Assigns do not within the space of three years next coming after the date of these Presents Cultivate & Improve three acres part of every fifty of the Tract above mentioned, then the Estate hereby granted shall Cease and be utterly Determined & thereafter it shall & may be Lawful to & for us, our Heirs & Successors to grant the same Lands & Premises with the Appurtenances, unto such other Person or Persons as we, our Heirs & Successors shall think fit.

In Witness Whereof we have Caused these our Letters Patent to be made.

Witness our Trusty ₁& welbeloved John, Earl of Dunmore, our Lieutenant & Governor General of our said Colony & Dominion at Williamsburg, under the seal of our said Colony the fifteenth Day of December one Thousand seven hundred and seventy two in the thirteenth Year of our Reign.

Meanwhile the Crown had itself followed Dinwiddie's example. George III's proclamation of October 7, 1763,[80] which framed the government of the lands ceded by France in the treaty of Paris (February 10, 1763) contained also the following provision:

'And whereas we are desirous upon all occasions to testify our royal sense and approbation of the conduct and bravery of the officers and soldiers of our armies and to reward the same, we do hereby command and empower our governors of our said provinces on the Continent of North America to grant without fee or reward to such reduced officers as have served in North America during the late war, and to such private soldiers as have been or shall be disbanded in America and are actually residing there and shall personally apply for the Same, the following quantities of lands subject at the expiration of ten years to the same quit rents as other lands are subject to in the provinces within which they are granted and also subject to the same conditions of cultivation and improvement, viz:

Field officers	5,000 a.
Captains	3,000 a.
Subalterns	2,000 a.
Non coms.	200 a.
Privates	50 a.'

Under this provision several grants of Virginia lands were

duly made. The third William Byrd, who had served as Colonel of the Virginia Regiment, made a claim in his own behalf in August, 1764, followed by another in December, 1768, on behalf of his officers, seeking patents within the bounds of the 'lands dately purchased of the Six Nations' by the treaty of Fort Stanwix.[81] One of the patents, which issued in due course, was as follows:[82]

[Dunmore's patents in pursuance of the Royal proclamation of 1763]

George the third by the Grace of God of Great Britain, France and Ireland, King Defender of the Faith &c.

To All to Whom these Presents shall come—Greeting.

Whereas by our Royal Proclamation dated at Saint James' the Seventh daye of October one thousand seven hundred and Sixty three in the third Year of our Reign For Regulating the Cessions made to us in America by the last Treaty of peace We did Command and Impower our Governors of our Several Provinces in North America to grant without fee or reward to such reduced Officers as had served in North America during the late War and to such private Soldiers as had been or should be disbanded in America and are actually residing there and should personally apply for the same certain Quantities of Land Subject at the expiration of ten Years to the same Quit Rents as other Lands are Subjected to;

And it being sufficiently proved to our Lieutenant and Governor General of our Colony and Dominion of Virginia that John Connolly late a Surgeons Mate in the General Hospital of our Forces in America is entitled to two thousand Acres of Land under our Royal Proclamation aforesaid,

Know ye therefore that for the Consideration aforesaid We have Given, Granted and Confirmed and by these Presents for us our Heirs and Successors Do Give, Grant and Confirm unto the said John Connolly one Certain Tract or Parcel of Land Containing two thousand Acres lying and being in the County of Fincastle on the South side of the Ohio River opposite to the falls thereof and bounded as followeth . . .

With all Woods, Under Woods, Swamps, Marshes, Lowgrounds, Meadows, Feedings and his due Share of Veins, Mines and Quarries as well discovered as not discovered within the bounds aforesaid and being part of the said Quantity of two thousand Acres of Land and the Rivers, Waters and Water Courses therein Contained together with the privileges of hunting, Hawking, Fishing, Fowling and all other profits, Commodities and Hereditaments whatsoever to the same or any part thereof belonging or in any wise Appertaining.

To Have, Hold, Possess and Enjoy the said Tract or parcel of Land and all other the before Granted Premises and every part thereof with their and every of their appurtenances unto the said John Connolly and his Heirs and Assigns forever to the only use and behoof of the said John Connolly, his Heirs and Assigns forever.

To be Held of us, our Heirs and Successors as of our Manor of East Greenwich in the County of Kent in free and Common Soccage and not in Capite or by Knights Service,

Yielding and Paying unto us, our Heirs and Successors for every fifty Acres of Land and so proportionately for a lesser or greater Quantity than fifty Acres the Fee Rent of one Shilling Yearly to be paid upon the Feast of Saint Michael the Arch Angel [September 29] next after ten Years from the date of these presents and also Cultivating and Improving three Acres part of every fifty of the Tract above mentioned within three years after the date of these presents.

Provided always that if three Years of the said Fee Rent from and after the expiration of the ten years aforesaid shall at any time be in arrear and unpaid, or if the said John Connolly his Heirs or Assigns do not within the space of three years next coming after the date of these presents Cultivate and Improve three Acres part of every fifty of the Tract above mentioned, then the Estate hereby Granted shall Cease & be utterly Determined; and thereafter it shall and may be lawful to and for us our Heirs and Successors to grant the same Lands and Premises with the Appurtenances unto such other person or persons as We our Heirs and Successors shall think fit.

In Witness Whereof We have Caused these our Letters Patent to be made.

Witness our Trusty and welbeloved John Earl of Dunmore our Lieutenant and Governor General of our said Colony and Dominion at Williamsburg, under the Seal of our said Colony the Sixteenth day of December one thousand seven hundred and Seventy three, in the Fourteenth Year of our Reign.

CHAPTER TWO

THE NORTHERN NECK GRANT BOOKS

§ 1. *The Constitution of the Proprietary*

CHARLES I was beheaded at Whitehall on January 30, 1648/9. When the news reached Virginia, that Dominion, unshaken in its loyalty, at once proclaimed his son as Charles II, invited his followers to cross the Atlantic 'as to a place of refuge,' and, as Clarendon further testifies, 'almost' invited Charles himself. Thus it was that in September, 1649, although an exile in France, the prince was indubitably King of Virginia, for there the government was carried on in his name. The motto adopted by the Virginia Company in 1619 might now have been modified to read *En dat Virginia solum*.[83]

At St. Germain-en-Laye the new King was surrounded by a little group of faithful cavaliers, whose individual losses consequent upon their service to his father, as well as to himself, certainly deserved the gratitude of the House of Stuart and demanded whatever compensation its chief had in his power to bestow. Charles II recognised this obligation and, exercising the royal prerogative in respect to the Dominion which had admitted his power in the premises, granted to seven of these veterans all the unseated portion of Virginia's tidewater. What he did was altogether in the tradition of the 'military right' to frontier lands which the Virginia government itself had previously declared to be 'the Usual policy and custom of all Nations, but in more espetiall manner of the state of England.' So the proprietary of the Northern Neck of Virginia came into existence.[84]

In response to Governor Berkeley's invitation, two of the patentees embarked for Virginia. They planned to take possession of the estate and fulfill the implied condition subsequent of promoting development. When they arrived the little

colony of Maryland refugees at Chicacoan had only just
begun to take out Virginia patents. It is fair to assume that
if the proprietors had then been able to make a substantial
show of exercise of their rights they would have prevented
the opposition which was to disappoint their expectations a
decade later. Virginia would doubtless have protested, as she
did against Lord Baltimore, but the logic of the situation would
have been against her. The representatives of the proprietors
had, however, hardly arrived in Virginia before a fleet sent
out for the purpose by the English Parliament succeeded in
ousting the royal government and, in doing so, suspended the
new proprietors' claim.[85] As a consequence the Northern Neck
charter was without vigor.

Immediately after the Restoration the survivors of the
patentees refreshed their title. They enrolled in chancery the
charter of 1649 and again made plans to take possession of
the territory therein described. To that end they sent Sir
Humphrey Hooke to America, armed with a royal letter addressed to the Governor of Virginia, instructing him to aid
the proprietors in 'settling the plantations and receiving the
rents and profits thereof.'[86]

Berkeley found himself practically powerless to give effect
to these instructions. Since the charter issued, the conditions
had changed. The Northern Neck was now no longer 'waste'
land. During the Commonwealth many new immigrants to the
colony, as well as some 'ancient planters' from the lower tidewater, had seated boundaries on the banks of the Potomac and
the Rappahannock, had taken out individual head right patents,
and Northumberland, Lancaster and Westmoreland had been
organized. Despite the declaration of the King's letter to
Berkeley that there was no intention of the Crown to with-
draw 'the said Plantation from under the care of the Governor
and Council of Virginia,' these settlers were suspicious of
being included in another politically separate palatinate like
Maryland; as, indeed, was not unjustified by the explicit provisions of the charter of 1649 for feudal jurisdictions. Taking
their cue from these provisions, the lawyers in the colony

revived the midieval doctrine that the obligations on which the feudal law was founded prohibited their 'lord' from alienating land which they held immediately of him, as much as it prohibited them from transferring their fealty to another. This was enough for the planters; they refused to attorn to the representatives of the proprietors, and, securing sufficient support in the council to out vote Berkeley, procured the Virginia government to 'obstruct' their proceedings.

The proprietors were therefore compelled to appeal again to the Crown, when the Privy Council, seeking an accommodation, put them into negotiation with Francis Moryson, then the resident agent for Virginia in London. The result was one of the several notable diplomatic achievements of that able colonial ambassador. He made a treaty, under which the proprietors surrendered the charter of 1649 and took out a new one, dated May 8, 1669.[87] This instrument contained several new clauses, viz: (1) a specific recognition and confirmation of the titles to all Northern Neck plantations seated under head rights prior to Michaelmas (September 29), 1661, subject only to the right of the proprietors to such quit rents and escheats as Virginia had reserved in respect thereto; (2) a limitation of the title of the proprietors to such other lands as might be 'inhabited or planted at or by the means or payment of' the proprietors themselves 'within the tyme and space of one and twenty years now next coming,' i. e., prior to May 8, 1690; and (3) a recognition of the political jurisdiction of the Virginia government within the proprietary by qualification of the clauses of the original charter as to 'regalities.' In consideration of these substantial concessions Moryson undertook that Virginia should co-operate, and Berkeley's Council duly ratified his agreement. The Land Patent Books show that throughout all this discussion the local government had continued to issue head right patents for Northern Neck lands; but now, at the end of 1669, the steady flow of such patents ceased.[88] It is thus apparent that the Council was then preparing to assist the proprietors in setting up their own land office temporarily to take the place of that of the Virginia government as the source of new titles in the Northern Neck.

Before this settlement could be made effective, Virginia was thunderstruck by the grant of her entire territory to Lords Arlington and Culpeper by the charter of February 25, 1672/3.[89] This insult to the colony had an immediate and unexpected repercussion upon the fortunes of the proprietors of the Northern Neck. The passions which blazed against the new proprietors did not spare the old. Berkeley and his Council themselves lit the flame. Publicly before the people they denounced the derogations from their authority which were implicit in the Arlington charter. Particularly, they laid stress upon the transfer to 'particular persons' of the entire function of granting waste lands in the colony, as well above as below the Rappahannock. As a warning against resort to the land office which it was expected Lord Arlington would attempt to set up, they cast doubt upon all proprietary titles.

'The demise being for the term of 31 years,' they said, '[the proprietors] hath yet power of granting lands in fee simple; which being contrary to law may deceive those who shall sue out such grants; since the foundation of their title being illegal they may be ousted of their possession after they have laid out their estates, after duties upon them; and consequently ruined.'[90]

While the Northern Neck charter of 1669 contained no such defect as this, it can be appreciated that after the members of the Council had warned the planters against taking Arlington grants because of the want of power of that noble lord to grant an estate of inheritance, the average man, not being a conveyancer, was unlikely to discriminate between what he had been specifically warned against and what the proprietors of the Northern Neck offered. One can almost hear the oracular wisdom uttered in a group of planters gathered in 1674 for (say) Stafford Court, that of course there was no difference in the legal limitations of the two charters for had not Squire Moryson cut down the Northern Neck charter also to one and twenty years! and any way all proprietors were papist rogues!!

In this situation the Northern Neck proprietors went a third time to the Privy Council, complaining that their representatives were still 'interrupted in planting and settling said territory.'[91] The King sent a sharp order in their behalf. This was duly filed with the Council by Thomas Kirton, the proprietors' agent, but it had now become impossible to restore local confidence.[92] Conscious of his own part in this result, Berkeley suggested to the Assembly that an offer be made to buy out the Northern Neck at the same time that representations were pending at court on the subject of the Arlington grant, and offered, himself, to lend the colony £1200 to accomplish that relief from one horn of the dilemma.[93] He had doubtless been advised that the weary proprietors were quite ready to quit, for they promptly named their price as £400 a piece for the six shares in which the charter was then held. Thereupon Virginia applied to the Crown for a charter of incorporation to enable her to make the purchase. At the very brink of accomplishment the negotiations collapsed with the outbreak of Bacon's Rebellion, when all concerned in Virginia were diverted to more serious affairs.[94] And so it was that the proprietary remained suspended in the air until after Lord Culpeper had played his part on the stage of Virginia history.

Although his father had been one of the patentees of 1649, Thomas, Lord Culpeper, did not on the Restoration assert any claim in that respect and it does not appear that he had any stake in the proprietary until 1673. His interest in Virginia had its origin in his appointment, in March, 1671, and subsequent active service, as a member of the 'Council for Foreign Plantations,' during which he seems to have learned enough of the colony to see in it an opportunity to collect the debt of £12,000 which was due him from the Crown on a grant made to his father immediately after the Restoration. It was to that end that he invoked the potent partnership of Lord Arlington and solicited the charter of 1673 which proved so obnoxious to Virginia. Contemporaneously he obtained also a patent for the governorship and a recognition by the proprietors of the Northern Neck of him and his cousin, Alexander Culpeper, as each entitled to a one-sixth interest in that Virginia estate as of the rights of their respective fathers as original patentees.[95]

As an incident of his triple interest in the colony, Culpeper became the managing partner of the proprietary. It was in that capacity that he sealed in March, 1674/5, the earliest Northern Neck grant.

This was intended to be a test of the powers of the proprietors. The grantees were Nicholas Spencer and John Washington of Westmoreland. The consideration is not recited, but, although (Beverley says) Spencer was Culpeper's cousin, it was not love and affection which caused him to vest in two of the important Potomac River men of the time, a member of the Council and an influential burgess, a tract of land to which Richard Lee, another member of the Council and the leader in the local opposition to the proprietary interest, already laid a claim, confirmed by the Council as early as 1660, under earlier head right grants. Because of its combination of political and sentimental interest, this corner stone of George Washington's title to his Mount Vernon estate is here set out in full, viz.[96]

[The 'Mount Vernon' grant of 1675]

To all to whome these present shall come,
The Owners and Proprietors, of all that Tract and Terrytory of Land in Virginia in America. mentioned in his Majtys: Letters Pattent Under the broad Seale of England, bearing date the Eight day of May in the One and Twentieth Year of his now Majesty's reign

Send Greeting in our Lord God Everlasting.
Know Yee. that by Vertue thereof, and for and in consideration of the yearly Rent & agreements hereafter Expressed and reserved, Wee have Bargained, Sold, Released, and Confirmed, and doe by these Presents, under our common Seale; Bargain, sell, release and confirm unto *Coll. Nicholas Spencer, and Lieut: Coll: John Washington,* of Virginia in America, five thousd. acres of Land:

Situate, lying and being within the said terrytory in the County of Staffd. in the freshes of Potomack river, & near opposite to Pis-

catoway Indian town in Mariland, and near the Land of Captn.
Giles Brent on the north Side, and near the land Survey'd for Mr.
Wm. Green, Mr. Wm. Dudley, and others on the South side: being
a neck of Land. bounded, betwixt two Creeks and the main river: on
the East pte. by the sd. main river of Potowmack; on the north pte. by
a Creek called by the English Little Hunting creek. and the main branch
thereof; on the South pte. by a Creek. named and called by the
Indians, Epsewassen Creek. and the main branch thereof. which Creek
divides this Land of Green, and Dudley, and others; on the west
pte. by a right line drawn from the Branches of the aforesd. Epsewassen, and Little Hunting Creeks, including the aforesd. Quantity,

Together with all Woods, trees, Underwoods, proffittts commodi-
tys Emolumtts and hereditaments. whatsoever thereunto belonging (all
manner of mines of Gold, Silver and Copper. only Excepted. and
foreprized.)

To have and to hold. all and Singular the prmises (except before
excepted) to the sd. Coll: Nichs. Spencer, and Lieut. Coll. John
Washington. their heirs, and assigns for ever.

Yielding. and paying. therefore Yearly, and every year, the rent
of four Shills: of Lawfull money of England. for every hundd:
acres, and soe proportionably. for a Bigger or lesser Quantity, to
the Sd. Proprietors, our heirs, and assigns for Ever, Upon the first
day of Novemr. commonly called the feast of all Saints. at the
Court house of the County where the sd. Lands are Scituate, or
Such other. place within our sd. terrytory. as wee, or any or either
of us, shall direct and appoint from time to time; the first paymt:
thereof to be made on the first day of Novemr. now next ensueing.

Provided. always that if the sd. Coll: Nicholas. Spencer. and
Lieut. Coll: John Washington. their heirs, and assigns. doe Yearly.
and every Year. between the feast day of St. Michael the arch
angel. [September 29] and the said first day of November. pay or cause
to be pd. unto us the sd. Proprietors, our heirs, and assigns for ever, the
Yearly rent of two Shills: Sterlg: in Specia. for every hundred
acres. and Soe proportionately for a Bigger, or lesser Quantity, then
it shall be taken and accepted by us the sd. proprietors, our heirs,
and assigns. in full Satisfaction. of the four Shills: above mentioned,

Provided. that if the sd. Coll: Nicholas. Spencer and Lieut. Coll:
John Washington. their heirs, and assigns. shall not plant or Seat
the sd. Lands, or cause the Same to be Planted. or Seated. within the
term. of three Years. next ensuing. the date hereof, that then this
Grant & everything herein Contained shall be void and Null to all
Intents. and purposes whatsoever. as if the Same had never been made,

And lastly 'tis agreed. that this Grant be Registered. in due form
in Virginia. aforesd. by the said Coll Spencer. and Lieut. Coll John
Washington, or their Assigns, before the first day of November.
now next ensuing.

In witness whereof wee the sd. Proprietors have hereunto affixed our Common Seal, and caused the Same to be Counter signed. by one or more of us, in the name of the rest. this first day of March in the 27th. Year of the reign of our Sovereign Lord King Charles the Second, Annoq: Domini. 1674 [O. S.].

Tho. Culpeper
Antho. Trethewy[97]

Whereas it doth appear to us by a Survey Signed by Mr. John Alexander Surveyor, bearing date Aprill: the 27th: 1669. that he then Survey'd for Coll Nichos. Spencer, and Lieut. Coll: John Washington five thousand acres of Land. lying upon the freshes of Potomack. river. for wch. Said Land wee have passed a Patt. unto the Sd. Coll: Nicholas Spencer. and Lieut: Coll: John Washington, bearing date the first of this Instant. March.

You are hereby required. to pass. and Register the Same notwithstanding any Pretence. or Pretences, any person or persons either doth or Shall make to any part or parcell of the Sd. Land. be it either by the title. of Surveying, Seating or planting upon the Sd. Land, Since the aforesd. Land was Survey'd for the aforesd. Coll: Nichs. Spencer. and Lieut. Coll John Washington.

Given under our hands March the 9th. 1674 [O. S.].

To Mr. Wm. Aretkin
our Agent in Virginia

Tho: Culpeper
Antho: Trethewy

Recorded in the Court Records of Staffd. March the 12th. anno: Domini. 1690 By James Hare dep. Cl: Cur: Peticla 1690.

Immediately upon the death of Sir William Berkeley in July, 1677, Culpeper took the oath as Governor, and served as such until he forfeited his patent in August, 1683.[98] He was, however, in the colony actively exercising the function only during two brief tours, from May to August, 1680, and from December, 1682, to May, 1683. The historians of the period all record that on the first occasion his affability and apparent interest in their welfare won golden opinions from the planters, but that the second appearance was characterized by exhibitions of rapacity which disgusted all who came into contact with the administration. None of these writers provides a convincing explanation of this hardening of Pharaoh's heart. The fact seems to be that, encouraged by the success of his blandishments in 1680, Culpeper made up his mind that he could secure local acquiescence in an effective application of the two proprietary charters in which he was interested; and in order to reap the full harvest of such an achievement determined to buy out all the other proprietors. In any event, he duly made the purchases in the summer of 1681. His deed from the other proprietors of the Northern Neck was dated July 21st and that from Lord Arlington, September 10, 1681. Culpeper recorded these instruments in the General Court at once on his return to Virginia in December, 1682.[99]

He seems to have deemed it expedient to begin the assertion of these new rights in the Northern Neck. Reciting himself 'sole owner,' he proceeded to appoint a 'Receiver General' in each county of the proprietary and gave those officers the full backing of the government.[100] He was thus enabled to collect the local quit rents, but the greater profits which were expected from fines on new land grants were conspicuously lacking. No one in the Northern Neck entered for any new land: the jactitation of the proprietary title served only to stir the embers of old resentment and sullen opposition.

Culpeper's sudden return to England in May, 1683, (in some respects similar to that of Queen Elizabeth's Lord Essex, when he deserted his government in Ireland), may thus be explained by an appreciation that his investment in the two charters was likely to be a loss, and that his best opportunity to recoup was to be at court and there seek to sell his franchises either to the Crown or to the colony. In respect to the Arlington charter he was successful: in consideration of a pension of £600 per annum for 21 years charged upon the establishment of the army he surrendered that grant to the Crown by a deed dated May 27, 1684.[101] As to the Northern Neck, Culpeper's agents in Virginia were able contemporaneously to provoke the Assembly to request Lord Howard to open negotiations for a purchase by the colony on the basis of the agreement of 1675; but partly on the question of price and partly because Virginia still lacked the power to make the purchase in a corporate capacity, that business failed.[102]

The resourceful Culpeper then made another effort to give the Northern Neck charter vitality by exercising his undisputed function of creating manors within the territory. To that end he encouraged Messrs. Brent and Fitzhugh to make speculative surveys of waste lands. It was thus and at this time that there were carved out of the proprietary the two notable estates, later known as 'Ravensworth' and 'Brent Town,' the titles for which, like that of Culpeper's earlier 'Mount Vernon' grant, were to persist into the eighteenth century. Of these trial balloons, only Brent Town ripened into a grant by Culpeper himself. The instrument by which that grant was accomplished is in consequence of high interest among the eocene examples of the form of land title on which the Northern Neck was soon to flourish, and is here set forth in full as follows,[103] viz:

[The Brent Town grant of 1687]

This Indenture made the Tenth day of January Annoq Dom 1686 [o. s.] and in the second Year of the Reign of our Sovereign Lord James the second by the Grace of God of England Scotland France and Ireland King Defender of the ffaith &c Between the Right Honourable *Thomas Lord Culpeper* Baron of Thoresway in the Kingdom of England of the one part and *George Brent* of Woodstock of Stafford County in his Majestys Colony of Virginia upon the Continent of America; *Richard ffoote* of the City of London, Merchant; *Nicholas Hayward* of the same City, Notary publick; and *Robert Bristow* of the same City, Merchant, of the other part.

Whereas our late Sovereign Lord King Charles the Second by his Letters Patents under the Great Seal of England bearing date at Westminster the 8th day of May in the one & twentieth Year of His Reign Annoq Dom 1669 did for the Consideration therein Expressed give grant and Confirm unto Henry then Earl of St Albans John Lord Berkley of Stratton & Sr William Moreton Knight then one of the Justices of the King's Bench and John Trethewy Esq. their Heirs and Assigns for ever

All that entire Tract Territory or parcell of Land scituate Lying and being in America & bounded by and within the Heads of the Rivers Tappahanock als Rappahanock and Quiriough or Potowmack Rivers & Courses of the said Rivers as they were commonly called or known by the Inhabitants & discriptions of those parts & Cheaseapeck Bay *together* with the Rivers themselves and all the Islands within the Banks of those Rivers & all Woods under Woods Timber and Trees, ways Waters rivers ponds : pools watercourses fishings Streams havens ports harbours Creeks, Wreckes of sea fish, Royal Deer wild Beasts & Fowl of what Nature or kind soever,

mines of Gold & Silver tinn Iron Copper Quarries of stone and
Coale which then were or at any time hereafter shou'd be had,
coming, being Arising renewing accruing found or taken within the
bounds or precincts aforesaid together with the Royalties of Hawking & Hunting for themselves their Heirs and Assigns Servants and
Tenants in and upon the Lands & premisses aforesaid & upon every
part & parcel thereof *saving excepting and Reserving* unto his said
Majesty his Heirs & successors one full fifth part of all Gold Mines
& Gold Oar thereafter to be had & one full tenth part of all Silver
Oar thereafter to be had and found upon the said Territory or
tract of Land,

 To have hold & Enjoy all the said Entire tract territory or portion of Land & all & singular the premisses with their and every
of their appurtenances (except before Excepted) to the said Henry
Earl of St Albans John Lord Berkley Sr William Moreton & John
Trethewy their Heirs & Assigns for Ever to their only Use & behoof & to no other Use intent or purpose Whatsoever *Yielding &
paying* therefore Yearly at the ffeast of St John Baptist [June 24] to
our said Sovereign Lord his Heirs & Successors the sum of Six pounds
thirteen shillings & four pence at James Town in Virginia in Lieu
of all service & Demands whatsoever, With power to sell & alien
all the premisses or any part thereof to be holden of the said Grantees
as of any of their Manors in free & common Soccage in fealty only
& by suit of Court or by any other Lawfull Tenure or Tenures used
within the Kingdom of England Under & Subject to severall provisoes Conditions & Agreements therein mentioned as in & by the
said Letters patents, wherein are divers other Gifts Grants powers
priviledges & immunities, relation being thereunto had, more fully
and at large it doth & may appear, and,

 Whereas the Right title and Interest of in and to the said Lands
and premisses is by Deed Inroll'd and other sufficient Conveyances
in the Law Vested and come unto the said Thomas Lord Culpeper
who is become Sole Owner thereof to him and his Heirs for Ever

 Now this Indenture Witnesseth that the said Thomas Lord Culpepper for and in Consideration of a Competent Sum of Lawfull
Money of England to him in hand paid at and before the sealing
and Delivery hereof by the said George Brent Richard Foote Nicholas Hayward and Robert Bristow the Receipt Whereof the said
Thomas Lord Culpeper doth hereby Acknowledge and himself to be
therewith paid & satisfied and for and in Consideration of the Rents
Covenants Conditions and agreements hereinafter Contained on the
part and behalf of the said George Brent Richard Foote Nicholas
Hayward and Robert Bristow their Heirs and Assigns to be paid
done & performed and for other Good Considerations the said Thomas
Lord Culpepper thereunto moving hath granted bargained Sold re-
leas'd & Confirmed and by these presents Doth grant bargain sell
release & Confirm unto the said George Brent Richard Foote Nich-

olas Hayward and Robert Bristow their Heirs and Assigns for Ever

all that Tract Territory or parcel of Land Containing by Estimation thirty thousand Acres be the same more or less Scituate lying and being in or near the said County of Stafford in Virginia aforesaid Between the Courses of the said Two Rivers Rappahanock & Potowmack backwards at least six Miles Distant from the said Main Rivers and from any Land already seated and inhabited and upon and Between the South west and North east Branches of Ocaquan Creek and from thence towards the Mountaines *some part* or parcel of the said Tract of Land being now or late in the Tenure or Occupation of the said George Brent Richard Foote Nicholas Hayward and Robert Bristow or some of them, their or some or one of their Under tennants or Asisgns; and the said Granted Tract Territory or parcel of Land being part of the said Tract Territory or parcell of Land Granted or mentioned to be Granted by the said recited Letters patents.

And all Woods Under Woods Timber & Trees ways Water Courses ponds pools Waters fishings Streams Creeks Deer Wild Beasts and Fowl of what nature or kind soever and all Quarries of stone and Coal which now are or at any time hereafter shall be had coming being arising and renewing Accruing found or be taken within the Bounds precincts or Limits of the Lands heriditaments and premisses above mentioned or intended to be hereby Granted & Conveyed and all and singular Rights Royalties proffits perquisites Emoluments Tenements and Heriditaments whatsoever in the said Recited Letters patents mentioned or Contained or which can or may be taken held used or Enjoyed to and with the Lands and premisses abovementioned or intended to be hereby Granted and Convey'd or any part thereof, and the Reversion and Reversions, Remainder & Remainders Issues and profits of all and singular Lands hereditaments and promises herein before Granted or mentioned to be Granted and of Every part and parcel thereof and all the Estate Right title interest possession property Claim and Demand whatsoever of the said Thomas Lord Culpepper of in or to the same or any part or parcel thereof

Except & alwaies reserved unto the said Thomas Lord Culpepper his Heirs & Assigns out of this present Grant all Mines of Gold Silver Copper tinn & Lead with Liberty to digg take and carry away the same.

To have and to hold the said Lands heriditaments & premisses before in and by these presents Granted or mentioned or Intended to be granted and Conveyed with their & every of their Rights members & Appurtenances and every part and parcel thereof Except before Excepted Unto the said George Brent, Richard Foote Nicholas Hayward and Robert Bristow their Heirs and Assigns to the only proper Use and Behoof of the said George Brent Richard Foote Nicholas Hayward and Robert Bristow and of their Heirs and Assigns for Ever.

Yeilding and paying therefore Yearly unto the said Thomas Lord Culpepper his Heirs and Assigns, from and after the ffeast day of S. Michael the Arch Angel [September 29] next ensuing the Date hereof, the Sum of thirty pounds of Lawfull Money of England

at the Insureance Office upon the Royal Exchange London aforesaid,
at two ffeasts in the Year, that is to say S᷈ Michael the Arch Angel
[September 29] and the Anunciation of the Blessed Virgin Mary
[March 25], by even and equal portions; the first payment thereof
to be made upon the ffeast of the Anunciation of the Blessed Virgin
Mary [March 25] which shall be in the Year of our Lord God 1688
   provided always that it shall & may be lawfull to and for the
said Thomas Lord Culpepper his Heirs and Assigns within the space
of seven Years now next Ensuing to Survey and measure the said
Granted Lands & premises and if upon a due Survey and admeasurement to be made within the time aforesaid there shall be any overplus of Land above the said Thirty thousand Acres hereby intended
to be granted that then there shall be yielded & paid Yearly and every
Year from the said ffeast of S᷈ Michael the Arch Angel [September 29]
which shall be in the Year of our Lord 1687 for Ever unto the said
Thomas Lord Culpepper His Heirs and Assigns the Sum of two shillings of Lawful Money of England for every One hundred Acres of such
Overplus Land and after and according to the same Rate for a Greater
or Lesser Quantity than one hundred Acres thereof to be paid at
the place and on the ffeasts aforesaid by Even and equal proportions
   provided also that if upon the said Survey and admeasurement
the said Granted Lands & premises shall happen to be deficient and
wanting in the said Measure of thirty Thousand acres then there
shall be abated and allowed Yearly from the said Feast of S᷈ Michael
the Arch Angel [September 29] which shall be in the Year 1687 for
Ever out of the said Yearly Rent of thirty Pounds hereby Reserved the
Sum of two Shillings of Lawfull Money of England for every One hundred Acres of Deficient Land and after and according to the same rate
for a Greater or lesser Quantity than an hundred acres thereof to
be abated and allowed at the ffeasts aforesaid by even and equal proportions
   provided also that the Lands and premisses hereby Granted and
Conveyed shall be only Charged and Liable to pay the said Yearly
Rent of Thirty Pounds and that none of the persons of them the
said George Brent Richard Foote Nicholas Hayward and Robert
Bristow nor of their respective heirs Exrs or Admrs or any of them
shall be any ways Charged or Incumber'd with the payment thereof
or any part thereof
   provided always that if it shall happen that the said Yearly Rent
of thirty pounds or any part thereof to be behind or unpaid by the
space of six Calendary Months next after Either of the ffeasts aforesaid whereon the same ought to be paid as aforesaid being Lawfully
Demanded that then there shall be forfeited and paid unto the said
Thomas Lord Culpepper his Heirs & Assigns for every such default

the sum of five pounds of Lawfull Money of England (nomine poene)

and if the said yearly Rent of Thirty Pounds and the said Nomine poene of five pounds shall be behind and unpaid by the space of nine Months next after either of the ffeasts aforesaid, that then it shall and may be Lawfull to and for the said Thomas Lord Culpepper his Heirs and Assigns into the said Granted Lands and premisses or into any part or parts thereof to Enter and to have hold & enjoy the same and to take and Receive the Rents issues and proffits, thereby to raise satisfy and pay the said Rent and Nomine poene and every part thereof and all arrears thereof and all Costs Charges & Damages concerning the same and

Lastly it is declared & agreed by & between the said George Brent Richard Foote Nicholas Hayward and Robert Bristow for them and their Heirs that they will from henceforth stand and be seized of all the said Granted or mentioned to be Granted Lands Heriditaments and premisses with their appurtenances to and for the several and Equal Use and benefit of them the said George Brent Richard Foote Nicholas Hayward and Robert Bristow and of their several respective Heirs & Assigns for Ever as Tenants in Common and not as joint Tenants without any advantage to be had or taken by them or any of them by right of Survivorship by reason of their joint Estate in the premisses

In Witness whereof the parties above named to these present Indentures Interchangeably have set their Hands & Seals the Day & Year first above Written.　　　　　　Tho Culpepper.

Sealed with his Seal under Appendix Recogn. p. prefat. Thoma Dom. Culpepper 11° die Januarij 1686 Coram me Mgro Cancae:

Ja Astry

Sealed & Delivered by the within named Thos Lord Culpepper in presence of us

Wm Norrington
Mark Alder
Phineas Barbinett
Ant Wright, Nrius Publus

This Deed of State was Acknowledged in the County Court of Stafford by Mr William Fitzhugh attorney of the within named Thomas Lord Culpepper unto the Within named Capt. Geo Brent Mr Richard Foote Nicholas Hayward and Robert Bristow this 13th day of July Anno Dom. 1687 and was then Recorded

Cop: Test:　　　　　　　　Thos Claiborne Cl Cur.

If Culpeper did not realize on his investment in the Northern Neck, he succeeded in making the opportunity for his descendants to do so.[104] When the period of twenty-one years, limited in the charter of 1669, was about to expire, he represented to James II that by reason of the unexpected local obstructions he had been unable to reduce to possession such an estate as Charles II had intended to vest in his ancestors: he urged, therefore, that the original opportunity should be renewed to him. The argument was plausible and on September 27, 1688, there was sealed in Culpeper's sole name the third and final Northern Neck charter.[105]

Apparently King James intended by this instrument simply to reinstate his brother's bounty by wiping out all limitations as to time. The reservations of the political jurisdiction of the Virginia government, which Francis Moryson had procured, were meticulously protected, and proved to be effective when later some of them were challenged;[106] but subsequent judicial interpretation proved also that by introducing a few words into the original description, which the charter of 1669 had carried forward from that of 1649, Culpeper succeeded in materially enlarging what, in Virginia, were deemed the boundaries of his domain.

The amended description of the territory granted read as follows:

'All that entire Tract, Territory or Parcel of land situate, lying and being *in Virginia* in America and bounded by and within the *first* heads *or Springs* of the Rivers of Tappanhanocke alias Rappahanocke and Quiriough alias Patawomacke Rivers, the Courses of the said Rivers, *from their said first heads or Springs*, as they are commonly called and known by the Inhabitants and Descriptions of those Parts, and the Bay of Chesapoyocke, together with the said Rivers themselves and all the Islands within the *outermost* Banks thereof, *and the Soil of all and Singular the Premisses.*'

The additions to the old description, here indicated by italics, could only have been suggested by Culpeper's personal knowledge of the geography of Virginia.

The qualification in the description of the Northern Neck in the charters of 1649 and 1669, as to what was 'commonly called and known by the Inhabitants and Descriptions of those parts' was clearly intended only as an identification of the boundary rivers; but in Virginia it was promptly extended to apply also to the definition of the word 'heads' and so to limit the western boundary of the proprietary.

There has never been any local uncertainty as to what is the true Northern Neck. From the original division of Virginia into 'Necks' in 1608, as shown on the Smith map, the name Northern Neck was, as it still is, 'commonly' confined by 'the Inhabitants' to the peninsula bounded by the Potomac and the Rappahannock, which geologically is docked on the west by a line drawn from the falls of Rappahannock to the falls of Aquia. In 1649 this Neck was interposed between 'old' Virginia and what was then still believed to be Lord Baltimore's western boundary on 'Quiriough,' and it was probably all that the original proprietors thought they had acquired. But in 1661, when the proprietors first asserted their title, the vague geography of the Maryland and Northern Neck charters had been clarified by a general recognition that the true western boundary of Maryland was the Potomac as we know it today; and if a survey of the proprietary had then been made no one in Virginia could have disputed a western boundary on a line drawn from the falls of the Rappahannock to the falls of the Potomac, for those falls were what Virginia then knew as the 'heads' of the rivers. The explanation of this is found in a curious sea change which a simple geographical term had suffered in crossing the Atlantic.

In seventeenth century usage in England the 'head' of a stream connoted the fountain head, and that was what the conveyancers intended in drafting the charter of 1649; but in Virginia, where the settlements were still all on tidewater, the word had come to imply the head of navigation.[107]

Lord Culpeper's knowledge of the Virginia locution evidently brought home to him an appreciation that if in 1688 he repeated verbatim the description of the charter of 1649 and

1669, he ran a risk of having his proprietary interpreted as limited by the fall line of the boundary rivers. He therefore took no chance. By unmistakably defining 'heads,' in accordance with the English usage, as 'first heads or springs,' he saw that he could avoid the application of the 'commonly known' qualification to 'heads' standing alone.

The astuteness of this prevision was proved when at last in 1736 the determination of the bounds of the Northern Neck was for the first time undertaken. William Byrd, conscious of Virginia folk speech, then duly argued that the true boundary was at the fall line, but logically he was driven out of that position by the plea that the spread of population after 1688 had carried a practical recognition of the proprietary above the falls of both rivers. Still resting on the principle of his original interpretation, Byrd accordingly laid down on Mayo's map of 1737 the minimum western boundary as a line drawn 'from the Fork of Rappahannock to the Fork of Potomac,' i. e., from the mouth of Rapidan to the mouth of Shenandoah. This included most of the then outstanding proprietary grants and with them an area which Mayo estimated to be 1,476,000 acres.

As the consideration of the question by the Privy Council proved, such an interpretation might fairly have been made of the charter of 1649, but Culpeper's insertion in the charter of 1688 of 'first springs' as the definition of 'heads' concluded the question against Byrd: it remained to discover those 'first springs' in order to determine the bounds of the proprietary. Such a discovery, in 1736, revealed that Culpeper's description had pushed his western boundary across the Blue Ridge to the foot of the Alleghanies, and had enlarged the proprietary in the hands of Culpeper's grandson until it included, as Byrd reported, no less than 5,282,000 acres.

Culpeper did not long survive this achievement. Within three months from the date of his charter he was serving on the Committee of the House of Lords sent to invite the Prince of Orange to oust the King who had done him a favor. His ingratitude is apparent in Bishop Burnet's observation that he was the only one of that Committee who supported Halifax's proposal that William should be elected King in his own right. This was his last public appearance. Closing his career in attendance upon the Convention Parliament which placed William and Mary on the throne, Culpeper died at his house in St. James Street, London, January 27, 1688/9.[108]

The proprietary title was now again distributed among several individuals. Alexander Culpeper came forward to assert his claim to his undivided sixth as a tenant in common with Culpeper's heiress, and that lady, Catherine Culpeper, added to the list of proprietors by marrying Thomas, fifth Lord Fairfax.[109]

When the Assembly heard of the devolution, it seems to have been agreed that it offered a new opportunity to rid the colony of the proprietary. On August 1, 1690, Secretary Cole, writing on behalf of the local government, asked the aid of the earl of Shrewsbury. 'The present heirs,' he said,[110] 'having little prospect of profit, will probably make over their interest to the King on moderate terms.' The Governor, Lord Howard, being in England, also took a hand, and it was he who found that Lord Fairfax expected more than 'moderate terms.' Howard reported to the Council on Nevember 6th[111] that Fairfax said 'he could very hardly gett any part of what the other was sold for, soe had but little encouragement to part with this.' From this it appears that the new proprietors remembered what had been paid Lord Culpeper for his surrender of the charter of 1673.

Virginia then resorted to politics to push the point. It was assumed that the new proprietors lacked the personal influence which Culpeper himself had persistently exercised at court, and that a frontal attack on them might find support in the current political sentiments of hostility to all the last acts of James II. Accordingly, in May, 1691, a vigorous petition, praying the Crown to resume the Northern Neck charter, was addressed to William and Mary.[112] To its surprise, the colony found that it had caught a Tartar.

It may have been known in Virginia that Culpeper had declared for William III; but it probably was not known that Lord Fairfax also had taken an active part in the Revolution of 1688, and in consequence was potent in the new regime. Moreover, Culpeper's widow, a vigorous woman, rose to the defence of her daughter's inheritance. Together they countered upon Virginia with a peteition of their own, praying that the current innuendos of irregularity in the procurement of the charter of 1688 be investigated and, if disproved, that the charter be confirmed. The Privy Council referred the two petitions to the Attorney General (Sir John Somers) and he, having examined the record and heard counsel for both parties, reported that there was no ground 'for vacating the said Letters Patents by *scire facias* or otherwise.' On this report an Order in Council was entered on January 11, 1693/4:[113]

'That the Pet^rs Margaret Lady Culpeper, Thomas Lord Fairfax, Katherine his wife and Alexander Culpeper, Esqr be permitted to enjoy the said Letters Patents according to Law, so as they keep strictly to the Tenor thereof, in Execution of the several powers and authorities thereby granted; of which all Persons whom it may concern are to take notice.'

This decree closed the first chapter of the history of the proprietary by definitely establishing it.

§2. *The Agents and their Records*

By reason of the loss of the books of the General Court[114] the earliest proprietary agents have become dim ghosts. The list should begin with the several representatives sent successively to Virginia by the syndicate of Bristol merchants, who, under the leadership of Sir Humphrey Hooke, took a lease of the proprietary in 1662 from the original patentees, but the scant surviving testimony for that fruitless adventure does not supply their names.[115]

The real records of the agency begin, therefore, with the establishment of a proprietary office in the colony after the issue of the charter of 1669.

1670-1673. *Thomas Kirton, agent.*
Land Office in Northumberland.

The lost Council Journal bore witness that in 1670 Thomas Kirton (a Somersetshireman, of kin to the Trethewys who had acquired Lord Hopton's interest in the Northern Neck pro-- prietary, and to Henry Norwood the non-resident Treasurer of Virginia) appeared at Jamestown and submitted a procuration to represent the proprietors in the colony. He was well received and began his work auspiciously enough. The recitals of some of the earliest recorded Northern Neck grants show that by 1672 he was commissioning surveyors and had opened an office at which entries were received. A minute of Northumberland court adds the detail that this office was in that county. But these bare facts complete Kirton's record in relation to the proprietary, for when Lord Culpeper assumed the management in 1673 he superseded Kirton by appointing William Aretkin.[116]

1673-1677. *William Aretkin, agent.*

For Kirton's successor the only evidence is the warrant addressed to him by Lord Culpeper in March, 1674/5, as 'our agent in Virginia,' directing him to 'pass and register' the grant then made to Nicholas Spencer and John Washington, of the lands which later became Mount Vernon.[117]

1677-1689. *Daniel Parke and Nicholas Spencer, agents.*
Land Office at 'Nomini' in Westmoreland.

Soon after Lord Culpeper qualified as Governor of Virginia, and while he still expected to be allowed to exercise his function by deputy, he gave a power of attorney to two leading men in the colony, Daniel Parke of York, and Nicholas Spencer of Westmoreland, 'to receive his dues.' The brief surviving note of this instrument shows that it was dated October 6, 1677,[118] and indicates that it included authority to collect quit rents under the Arlington charter as well as on behalf of the proprietors of the Northern Neck. Through Culpeper's continuing influence Parke was appointed Secretary of State a year later, but soon died,[119] when Spencer succeeded to the office of Secretary, which like the Northern Neck agency, he was to serve for a decade.

Spencer was an eminently fit man for this responsibility. Not only did he live and maintain his office in the proprietary, but already he had experience in the ticklish problems of its public relations by virtue of his contest with Richard Lee for the possession of the land which became Mount Vernon. More than that, his official dispatches reveal him to have been better educated than most of his generation in the colony, as well as cool and cautious in business; but he was unable to make anything of the Northern Neck. Beverley's observation that he 'did but little in his Lordship's service and only gain'd some few strays that used to be claimed by the Coroner in behalf of the King,' is confirmed by the recitals of Spencer's proceedings with relation to the proprietary, which appear in the subsequent grant books and the county records. He continued, however, to act as Culpeper's 'agent and attorney' until the end of his life, surviving his principal by only a few months.[120]

It remained, therefore, for Culpeper's successors to establish the proprietary on a working basis. The Northern Neck Grant Books which survive in the Land Office at Richmond in unbroken series down to the American Revolution, were opened by their procurement in August, 1690.

1690-1693. *Philip Ludwell, agent, N. N., 1.*
Land Office in Westmoreland.

As Spencer's successor, the new proprietors chose 'another noted Gentleman, an old Stander in that country, Col. Philip

Ludwell,' who had recently become their kinsman by marrying Alexander Culpeper's sister, the widow of Sir William Berkeley.[121] Ludwell was in England in the autumn of 1689, agitating his and the Assembly's quarrel with Lord Howard of Effingham, which had resulted in his most recent removal from the Virginia Council. His popularity in the colony, demonstrated by his assignment to that duty, as well as his parts, seem to have commended him to all the contemporary holders of proprietary charters in America: when he returned to Virginia he brought with him both the Northern Neck agency and a commission to be Governor of the Albemarle colony in North Carolina. As this last responsibility was satisfied by the administration, by deputy, of the turbulent settlement which lay below Virginia's southern border, Ludwell could, and did, himself remain at home at 'Greenspring' in James City and from that vantage drive both his new horses.

Ludwell had offended Lord Howard and for that reason at once faced in the Northern Neck a dogged opposition from the Virginia government. He seems, however, to have had, under cover, a fair measure of support from the county courts, and he fought the hostile influence of the Council with vigor and energy. His activities among the planters were disturbing enough to make the government squeal: Secretary Cole reported to the Lords of Trade, somewhat darkly, that his proceedings 'will probably lead to disturbance.'[122]

It was in the summer of 1690 that Ludwell began to put the proprietors' house in order. In October the Council warned the County Courts to have nothing to do with him and to return to the Secretary all papers he might have filed with them for record.[123] The return of Westmoreland Court to this order[124] shows that the proprietors' office had been re-established in Westmoreland (probably at Nicholas Spencer's house on Nomini,[125] but a certain record in that respect is lacking); that Richard Whitehead of Gloucester had been put in charge of it,[126] with Spencer's son, Nicholas, jr., and his nepehew, Francis Wright (the latter being then Sheriff of the county)[127] as deputies; and that an orderly system of receiving entries for 'waste' land and for making grants had been inaugurated. The minute of this return, adopted January 29, 1690/1, was as follows:

'In obedience to the Rt. Honorable the Lt. Governor, his commands we hand unto the Clerk of the County to transcribe coppies from the records of all such papers as have been published and recorded in our Court relating to Philip Ludwell, Esq., as agent or attorney of the Lord Culpeper, or any p'son authorized under him. Some other papers were sent to our Court with request to be published, of which we took no notice, which papers we have also, with the said coppies, ordered our Clerk to return herewith. Some office papers were published at our Court by Col. Ludwell or ordered when in our County, but not recorded, coppies of which we could not demand, for that Mr. Richard Whitehead who acts as Clerk of the Proprietors' office hath been absent from the said office sometime before Xmas last; but we doe not know nor find that any p'son hath acted by virtue of any power from the said Coll. Ludwell, except the said Mr. Whitehead, who made enries of land for all such p'sons as repaired to him for the same; and that Mr. Nicholas Spencer and Mr. Francis Wright to be his under agents for this County, which said deputation wee are informed is delivered up again.'

Beverley's statement, comparing Ludwell with Nicholas Spencer, that 'he likewise could make nothing of it,' is, therefore, rather rhetorical than the whole truth. Ludwell's record of grants shows a substantial achievement on behalf of the proprietors; and his failure of that complete success which ultimately crowned the efforts of Robert Carter in the same duty, may be attributed not so much to the agent himself as to the lack of tact of Richard Whitehead. William Fitzhugh testified to this specifically. 'The proprietors' interest,' he wrote to Roger Jones in 1693, 'at present lyes under very great confusion and distraction by reason of the incapacity of Coll. Ludwell's Deputy, and the opposition of the Government very ill managed.'[128]

Ludwell derived his authority to make grants from a procuration executed, probably in the autumn of 1689,[129] by Catherine and Alexander Culpeper, which vested in him 'full power and authority to act in the premises pursuant to the powers granted by their said Majesties, as fully and amply, to all intents and purposes, as they, the said Proprietors, themselves, might or could do it they were personally present.'

When he opened his land books in August, 1690, he accordingly described the proprietors as

'The Honorble Mrs. Katherine Culpeper, sole Daughter and heire of the said Thomas late Ld. Culpeper, and Alexander Culpeper, Esqr., who cometh in part proprietor by lawfull conveyance from Thomas late Lord Culpeper and confirmed by the sd. Mrs. Katherine Culpeper.'

So long as he continued in office he used the following form:[180]

[Philip Ludwell's form, 1690]

Whereas King Charles the Seacond of Ever Blessed Memory by his Letters Pattents Under the Broad Seale of England beareing date at Westminster the Eighth day of May in the one and twentyeth yeare of his Reigne Annoqe Dom. 1669, His Matie was Gratiously pleased to give Graunt and Confirme Unto Henry then Earle of St. Albons John Lord Berkley Sir William Morton Knt. & John Trethewy Esqr. there heires & assignes All that Intire Tract Territory or parcell of Land Lyinge & being Betweene the two Rivers of Rapah. and Patomack and the Courses of the said Rivers and the Bay of Chesapeake, as by the Said Graunts, Recourse beinge had there Unto, will more at Large appeare, and

Whereas all the Rite and Title of in and to the Said Lands & Premisses Is by Deed Enrold and other Suffentient Conveyance in Law Conveyed and made over to Thomas Lord Culpeper, Eldest Sonn & heire of John Late Lord Culpeper, his heires & assignes for Ever, who is thereby become Sole Owner and Propriator of the Said Land in Fee Symple, and

Whereas Kinge James the Seacond hath beene Gratiously pleased by his Letters Pattents Bearinge Date at Westminster the 27th day of September 1688, And in the fourth yeare of his Maties. Reigne, to Confirme the Said Graunt for the Said Tract or parcell of Land to the Said Thomas Lord Culpeper his heires & assignes for Ever, as by the said Graunt, Relation beinge there unto had, will more at Large appeare

And the Said Thomas Lord Culpeper he beinge Since Deceased all the Rite Title and Interest of in and to the Said Tract of Land Lawfully Desendinge on the Honorble. Mrs. Katherine Culpeper Sole Daughter and heire of the said Thomas late Lord Culpeper, And Allexander Culpeper Esqr. who Cometh in part propriator by Lawfull Conveyance from Thomas late Lord Culpeper, and Confirmed by the Said Mrs. Katherine Culpeper, who are thereby now become the true and Lawfull Propriators of the Said Tract or Territory, and

Whereas the Said Propriators have thought fitt Under there hands & Seales to Depute me Phillip Ludwell Esqr. with full power and Authority to Act in the Prmisses. persuant to the powers Granted by there Said Maties. as fully & Amply to all intents & purposes as they the said Propriators them Selves might or Could Doe if they were Personally present,

NOW KNOW YEE therefore tht. I the Said Phillip Ludwell Esqr. by the powers & Authority to me given and Graunted as aforeSaid, Doe heareby, Under the Condetions & provisoes hereafter mentioned, Convey make over and assigne unto Mr. John Newton, gent. of Westmoreland County and Coll. William Fitzhugh of Stafford County, gent., Joyntly, a Certaine Tract of Land Lying and beinge in the County of Stafford Conteyneing two thousand one hundred and fifty Acres, . . .

Togeather wth. all Woods Waters or other trees, with all Profitts Comodityes Emolluments & Heraditaments, whatsoever to the said Land belonginge or in any wise apperteyninge, with all Rites & privilidges of Hawkinge, Huntinge, Fishinge & Fowlinge, with all Mines Mineralls on the sd. Land,

Exceptinge one fifth part of all Gold Mines or Gold Oare, and one tenth part of all Silver Mines or Silver Oare, arisinge or that shall hereafter be found on the said Land, Reserved by his matie;

And alsoe Excepted and Reserved, To and for the Use of the propriators there heires & assignes, one fourth part of all Gold Mines or Gold Oare and one fifth part of all Silver Mines or Silver Oare as aforesaid (besides what his Matie hath Excepted & Reserved) Togeather with one third part of all Tinn, Copper, Iron, Lead, Cole Mines or Oare that shall be found as aforesaid

TO HAVE HOLD and peaceably to possess occupy and Enjoy all the Singuler the before Resighted premisses and all and Singuler the Rites Members and appurtinences thereto belonginge to them the said Jno. Newton and Coll. William Fitzhugh there heires & assignes for Ever

Yeildinge & payinge yearly to the said Propriators there heires and assignes for Ever the Sume of two Shillinge Sterlinge mony for Every hundred Acres heareby Graunted, the which paymt. is to be made from yeare to yeare and Every yeare at or Upon the feast day of St. Michaell the Arch Angell or after Upon all Demands, Either in mony Sterlinge as abovesaid or in good Spanish Mony after the Rate of five Shillings for a peece of Eight; or, in Case mony Cannot be had, in as good tobacco as any is, or shall be, made Upon the said Land, with Caske, after the rate the Quitrents now are or hereafter shall be paid in the other parts of Virginia;

as alsoe well and truly payinge after the Rate of five Shillings as a fine for Every hundred Acres for all quantitys of Land that shall be taken up above one hundred Acres to Six hundred Acres; And for all quantitys of Land above Six hundred Acres after the Rate of tenn Shillings for Every hundred Acres; The which said mony is to be paid within Six Monthes after the Signeinge Sealinge and Deliveringe the Conveyance for the same, Either in Mony Sterlinge, Spanish mony after the Rate of five Shillings for a peece of Eight, or in good tobacco after the Rate of Six Shillings per hundred

Always provided that if the quitrents above Mentioned of two Shillings per hundred Acres or the fines for Lands heareby Graunted shall be Either Omitted or Reserved to be paid by or for the Space of two whole yeares at any tyme, that then it Shall and may be Lawfull for the said Propriators; there heires or assignes to Re-enter and take possession of the said Land without the Hinderance or Mollestion. of any person or persons soe Neglectinge or Refusinge to pay the said Quittrents or fine as abovesaid.

And Lastly it is provided that it shall and may be Lawfull for the propriators there heires or assignes at any tyme to Admeasure the Land heareby Graunted whereby the true Contents thereof may be knowne.

All which dues beinge well and truly paid, and all other Clauses and provisoes hearein Meantioned performed, the said Jno. Newton and Coll. Wm. Fitzhugh shall and may by force & Virtue of these prsents. from tyme to tyme and at all tymes for Ever heareafter Lawfully peaceably and Quietly have hold Use Occupy Enjoy and possess the Lands and other the above Bargained prmises. with the appurtinences Unto the only proper Use & behoof of the sd. John Newton and Coll. Wim. Fitzhugh there heires and assignes for Ever, without any Lawfull Lett, Suite, troble or Disturbance of or from them the said Propriators there heires or assignes or Either of them, or by there or Either of there Meanes Consent or Procurement.

IN WITNESS whereof I the Under Written Phillip Ludwell Esqr. in the Names and one the behalfe of the said Propriators to me Graunted to the effect aforesaid, have heareunto Sett my hand and the usual Seale appointed by the Propriators to this purpose, this 28th day of August, 1690.

Phill Ludwell.

This form is of particular interest in the history of the Northern Neck land titles. Compared with the earlier 'Mt. Vernon' and 'Brent Town' forms, it is the source of several precedents adapted by William Fitzhugh and passed on to Robert Carter to be incorporated in the final form of the Northern Neck grant. In his persistent use of his form Ludwell perpetrated, however, the first of the several mistakes in technical conveyancing ('occasioned,' as Governor Gooch was to say, 'by the distance between G. Britain and this Place') which it was necessary for a subsequent proprietor to cure in 1736. The recital of 'the Honorable Mrs. Katherine Culpeper' and Alexander Culpeper as the only 'true and lawful proprietors' ceased to be a correct designation when, soon after executing Ludwell's procuration, Catherine Culpeper (she herself spelled the Christian name with a C) took to herself a husband. By virtue of the law of coverture that husband then became a proprietor; his authority to sign should have been procured and should have been recited with his name. As was later recognised, all of Ludwell's grants after the marriage were defective by that omission, and thereby put the rights of the grantees in jeopardy.

The next succeeding agents duly corrected this mistake; but if Philip Ludwell made a serious blunder he undoubtedly planted, during his brief tenure of the Northern Neck agency, the seed from which the proprietors reaped a bountiful harvest in the next generation.

1693-1700.   *George Brent and William Fitzhugh, agents, N. N., 2.*

Land Office at 'Woodstock' in Stafford.

In 1691 the proprietors of Carolina enlarged Philip Ludwell's function by naming him Governor of South as well as North Carolina, and early in 1693 they required him to go to Charles Town to hold an Assembly. It thus became necessary for Ludwell to give up the Northern Neck agency. The proprietors of that territory thereupon turned over their business to another remote kinsman, George Brent of 'Woodstock,'[131] but in doing so associated with him, as a balance wheel, his law partner, William Fitzhugh of 'Bedford.'[132] The only surviving evidence of the date of their procuration is a letter written by Fitzhugh to Capt. Roger Jones[133] in December, 1693, from which it may be gathered that Fitzhugh was included on Jones' recommendation, viz:

'I received [yours] about the 3d Nov[r] and a small time after Capt. Brent and myself received the powers and instructions from the Proprietors, of which we gave you an account by a ship then ready to go, which I hope by this time you have received.'

This combination might fairly have been expected to be successful. While both agents had been identified with the administration of the proprietary during the futile days of local animosity against Lord Culpeper himself,[134] neither was involved in that personal quarrel between Ludwell and Lord Howard, which had set the new proprietors off on the wrong foot. On the other hand, within a few months after their agency began, Brent and Fitzhugh had the moral prestige of the Order in Council of January 11, 1693/4, which definitely ended all hopes that the Crown might resume the Northern Neck charter. Despite these advantages, the event showed that the new agency was to be not merely less of a success than Ludwell's, but actually a failure. This seems to have been due primarily to Brent.

Fitzhugh was the stronger character of the two and might have been expected to control the agency. The embodiment of common sense, he had long felt that, in the explosive atmosphere by which the proprietary was surrounded, the true policy of management was the English principle of progress by compromise; in 1683 and again in 1689 he had made specific proposals to that effect to Lord Culpeper, but now again he was unheeded.[135] Brent was at once impetuous and insistent on the letter of his principal's rights.

The new agents took up their work actively in the autumn

of 1694, when, following the Order in Council, Lord Fairfax procured a letter from the Lords of Trade to the Virginia Council, requiring that they be supported. These instructions were duly spread upon the Council minutes. Lord Howard was no longer a factor in the problem, and the way lay open for adroit management of the only remaining handicap, which was the jealousy of the local magnates. It soon became evident that Brent controlled the agency and was offending everybody in the country; how he accomplished the subordination of his partner does not appear, but it may be conjectured, on the face of the records, that he softened Fitzhugh's judgment by liberal grants from the escheats. And so instead of placating the local dignitaries, who could have made their task easy for them, the agents announced that unless the recalcitrant holders of head right patents immediately attorned, they might expect to have to pay a quit rent at a rate double that which had been customary. It was this threat which moved Robert Carter to his savage attack upon them in the Assembly in May, 1695.[136]

The injustice of Carter's taunts seems to have moved even Fitzhugh to anger. At all events, there was a scene in the Council chamber while Carter's Address to the Crown was on its legislative progress, when Brent and Fitzhugh took such a high line that they lost the support of all those who had been prepared to accept the situation. Governor Andros reported this incident to the Lords of Trade in his dispatch of June 4, 1695.[137]

'I must assure you that Lord Fairfax's agents, being negligent of their business, in order to colour their failures, became insolent without cause, and that the respect towards their employers procured them as easy censure as their offence would admit.'

And so, although the Brent and Fitzhugh agency was to endure for another five years that Greek chorus, Robert Beverley, could justly sum up their experience in the phrases: 'they succeeded no better than their predecessors.'

Brent and Fitzhugh had been given as broad powers as Ludwell exercised. By their procuration[188] they were

'fully impowered, in our names and on our behalf to do, perform and execute such matters and things as may be conformable to the powers and privileges to us in and by the letters pattent given and granted.'

Under this authority they opened their book of grants on October 1, 1694, 'at our office in Stafford County, within our said proprietary.' Sometimes they signed together, and sometimes individually, especially when they issued grants to one another, for they were consistently their own best customers. For that purpose they used a form evidently drawn by Fitzhugh, which materially simplified Ludwell's form. It may be conveniently illustrated by reproducing the 'Ravensworth' grant, which is interesting for its recitals and was one of those with which their book opened,[139] viz:

[Brent and Fitzhugh's form, 1694]

Margarett Lady Culpeper, Thomas Lord Fairfax, Katherine his wife and Alexander Culpeper Esquire, Proprietors of the Northern Neck of Virginia,
To all To whom these presents Shall come Send Greeting in our Lord God everlasting
Whereas Philip Ludwell esquire our former Attorney and agent in the year of our Lord one thousand six hundred and Ninety, did for us and in our Names grant to Lt. Colo. William Fitzhugh a tract of Land lying in Stafford County in the freshes of Potowmack within our said proprietory containing twenty one thousand Nine hundred and ninety six acres, which said Land was Surveyed and laid out the twenty eighth day of April one thousand six hundred and eighty four by Samuel Wye Surveyor in Stafford so qualified by Thomas Kerton, then agent to the first proprietors under whom we claim, for John Matthews and other persons; which being all dead long since the whole right of the said Survey appertaining to the said Matthews, and by him Sold to the said William Fitzhugh, by deed of conveyance dated the twenty second day of August one thousand six hundred and eighty five, and acknowledged in Stafford Court the Nineteenth of September next following; upon the Appearance of which right, and for such Composition as to him the said Philip Lud-

well Seemeth meet and Satisfactory by the Said William Fitzhugh then to him made, the aforesaid grant, did pass and was issued out of our then office as appears by Mr. Richard Whitehead's Account, who was then Clerk of our Office under our Said Agent, Charging the said William Fitzhugh the Office fees for the said deed of Conveyance; but by some accident the said deed of Conveyance being lost, at the Suit and request of him the said Colo. William Fitzhugh at our Office now made to renew, and Confirm his said Grant

Know Ye, therefore, for an in consideration of the aforesaid grant and the rents hereafter reserved, we have granted, and Confirmed, and by these presents do grant and Confirm to him the said William Fitzhugh

the before mentioned tract of twenty one thousand, Nine hundred and Ninety Six acres of Land, situate in Stafford County as above said, and bounded as followeth Viz, lying upon the runs of Accotinke, Mussell Creek run [and] on the South side of the run of Four Mile Creek . . .

together with all rights, profits and benefits to the same belonging, Royall Mines excepted, and the full third part of all Lead, Copper, tinn and Iron Mines, that shall be found thereon.

To have and to hold the said twenty one thousand, nine hundred and ninety acres of Land together with all rights, profits, and benefits to the same belonging, or in any wise appertaining, except before excepted, to him the said William Fitzhugh, his heirs and assigns forever; he the said William Fitzhugh, his heirs or assigns therefore

Yielding and paying to us our heirs and assigns, proprietors of the Northern Neck, Yearly and every Year, on the feast of Saint Michael the Arch Angell the fee rent of twenty one pounds nineteen Shillings and six pence Sterling money,

provided that if the said William Fitzhugh, his heirs or assigns shall not pay the before reserved annual rent so that the same or any part thereof shall be behind and unpaid for the Space of two whole years after the same shall become due that then it shall be lawful for us our heirs, assigns, Certain Attornies or agents into the above granted premises to reenter and to hold in our first right so as if this grant had never passed,

Given at our Office in Stafford County within our said proprietory under our Seal,

Witness &c. dated October the first one thousand six hundred and ninety four,

George Brent.

It will be observed that in describing the proprietors Brent and Fitzhugh began by reciting all those to whom the charter of 1688 had been confirmed by the Order in Council of January, 1693/4. Fortunately for the grantees, Lady Culpeper was therein named (though not recited) in her capacity as administratrix of her late husband, for within a few months after the opening of Northern Neck Grant Book No. 2 she became a proprietor in her own right, and the use of her name without qualification covered this capacity also.

Alexander Culpeper died in London at Christmas, 1694. He had been living for some years at Leeds Castle, superintending Lady Culpeper's affairs, and she buried him in the Culpeper chapel of Bromfield, appurtenant to her residence. His will made the following provision :[140]

'*Whereas* I am seized to me and my heirs of and in one full sixth part, the whole in six parts to be divided, of and in a certain tract of land in the Continent of America, called the Northern Neck of Virginia, lying between Rappahannock and Potomack rivers in Virginia, under and by virtue of a grant thereof formerly made by his late Majty, King James II, to the Rt. Honble Thomas Lord Culpeper, and his heirs forever, I do hereby give the said sixth part unto the said Rt. Honble Margaret Lady Culpeper, widow and relict of the said Rt. Honble Thomas Lord Culpeper, deceased, and to her heirs forever.'

The agents either did not learn of, or failed to note, this demise for so far as the record indicates they continued to recite Alexander Culpeper among the proprietors to the end of the century.[141] Thus by accident only was avoided another such vital mistake as Ludwell had made in failing to take note of Catherine Culpeper's marriage.

Brent died in the spring of 1699 and for the ensuing eighteen months Fitzhugh carried on the agency alone. It was during this period that the fortunes of the proprietors turned. For nearly seventeen years since Culpeper had acquired the sole title to the estate he and his family had waged an unceasing defensive war against the efforts of the local magnates in the Northern Neck to nullify their rights. While they were uniformly successful with the authorities in England, in any large sense the activities in their behalf by their successive resident agents, Spencer, Ludwell, Brent and Fitzhugh, had been locally unsuccessful. Now at last, at the very end of the century, the tide suddenly turned. Writing in 1703, or almost contemporaneously, Robert Beverley gave the only explanation which has survived. 'At last,' he says, 'Colonel Richard Lee [the second of the name], one of the Council, an inhabitant of the Northern Neck, privately made composition with the Proprietors themselves for his own land. This broke the Ice, and several were induced to follow so great an Example, so that by degrees they were generally brought to pay their Quit Rents into the hands of the Proprietors' agents.'

The nature of this arrangement made unnecessary any grant, and, in consequence the grant books are silent in respect to it. It would be in the account books of the proprietors that the evidence might be found to check against Beverley's statement, but none of those account books for this critical period is extant, and that loss is aggravated for the historian by the lack of Fitzhugh's correspondence in the final years of his life. It is, however, a fair inference that Fitzhugh had a hand in bringing about Richard Lee's composition. Left free by Brent's death to change the policy of the agency in dealing with the holders of the old head right patents to Northern Neck lands, his more adroit habit of mind leads us to the judgment that it was he who prepared the minds of both parties for the compromise which Lee negotiated direct with Lord Fairfax, and so necessarily in London.

If this conjecture is warranted, the proprietors owed more to William Fitzhugh than the Virginia tradition has recognised.

1703-1712. *Robert Carter, agent, N. N., 3 & 4.*
Land Office at 'Corotoman' in Lancaster.

Fitzhugh signed his last grant under date of June 18, 1700, and died in the following October. As soon as Lord Fairfax was advised, he consulted that oracle of the Virginia Coffee House in London, the greatest of the contemporary Virginia merchants, the elder Micajah Perry,[142] and invited counsel in the selection of a new agent. Perry nominated his friend and correspondent, Robert Carter of Corotoman, whom he had recently procured to be raised to the Virginia Council and whose growing power in the colony at this time caused Governor Nicholson to dub him 'King.'[143] Considering that Carter's influence had been the most potent single factor in the local opposition to the proprietary, both in and out of the Assembly, it was a shrewd choice.

When Col. Carter accepted the duty, his procuration was executed under date of April 28, 1702, and renewed to him all the powers of Brent and Fitzhugh.[144] In June, 1703, he reopened the proprietary books at his own house, 'Corotoman,' so establishing that 'office in Lancaster county within our said proprietary,' which is thenceforth notable in the annals of the Northern Neck. His earliest act was definitely to crystallize the form of the grant. He modified Fitzhugh's precedent, in several respects to be hereafter discussed, as follows:[145]

[Robert Carter's form, 1703]

Marguritt Lady Culpeper, Thomas Lord Fairfax and Catherine his wife Proprietors of the Northern Neck Virginia:

To all to whom this present Writing Shall Come Send Greeting in our Lord God Everlasting

Whereas Coll. George Mason of the County of Stafford upon his Suggestion of a Certain Quantity of Land belonging to us on the Lower side of Ocoquon River in the said County, below & near the falls thereof, not yet granted, did on the Seventeenth Day of August Last Obtain a Warrant from Our Office for Laying out the Same & having Now Returned a Survey Thereof under the hand of Thomas Gregg Surveyor

Know Yee Therefore that wee for and in Consideration of the Composition to us paid and the Annuall Rent hereafter Reserved have Given and Granted and do by these Psents. give and Grant unto the said Coll. George Mason all that Tract and parcell of Land bounded according to the said Survey as followeth . . .

Together wth. all Rights Members and Appurtenances thereunto belonging Royall Mines Excepted, and the full Third part of all Lead, Copper, Tinn, Coles & Iron Mines that shall be found thereon.

To Have and to Hold The said Seventy Nine acres of Land To·gether with all Rights Profitts & Benefitts to the Same belonging or in any Wise appertaining, Except before Excepted, to him the said George Mason his heirs and Assigns for Ever; he the said George Mason his heirs and Assigns therefore

Yielding & paying to us our heirs Assigns or to the Certain Attorney or Attorneys of the said Proprietors, or to the Certain Attorney or Attorneys of our heirs or Assigns Proprietors of the said Northern Neck, Yearly and Every Year, on the feast of St. Michaell the Arch Angell the fee Rent of one Shilling Sterling Money for Every fifty Acres of Land hereby Granted

Provided That if the said George Mason his heirs or Assigns shall not pay the before Reserved Annuall Rent Soe that the Same or any part thereof Shall be behind or unpaid for the Space of Two whole years, after the Same shall become due if Lawfully Demanded, that then it shall and may be Lawful for Us Our heirs or Assigns Certain Attorneys or Agents into the above Granted premises to Re-enter and hold the Same Soe as if this Grant had never passed.

Given at our Office in Lancaster County within Our Said Proprietory under our Seale

Witness Our Agent and Attorney fully Authoriz'd thereto; Dated the Third Day of March in the Third Year of the Reigne of Our Sovereign Lady, Anne by the Grace of God of England Scotland France & Ireland Queen Defender of the Faith &c. Annoq Domini 1704.

Robert Carter.

During Carter's first agency the grant books reflect not only the general acquiescence in the proprietary as a source of land titles, but the beginnings of that movement of population into the interior, which was to realize the value of the estate as a source of income to its owners.

On this last point there survives a significant scrap of evidence. Col. Carter opened the new era by asserting the claim that the proprietary included the Great Fork of the Rappahannock, and that claim, while disputed, precipitated a new effort by the Virginia government to buy out the proprietors. The Council certified to the Lords of Trade in 1708 that the proprietary was not worth, to the proprietors, in excess of £300 per annum, and William Blathwayt of the Treasury suggested to Lord Fairfax that it might be possible to negotiate with the Crown an exchange of the proprietary for one of those

surviving feudalities which give an occasional midaeval colour
to eighteenth century English records. On the representation
that 'the lott and cope, and office of Bergmaster in the wapen-
take of Wicksworth' in the county of Derby was then worth
£300 per annum, the proprietors were induced to petition the
Crown to be vested with it in lieu of the Northern Neck. But,
while the question was under consideration, Lord Fairfax had
a report from Robert Carter that the Northern Neck income
had grown to £584, 13s., 2d. for the year 1708, and that report
put an effective end to the negotiations. The proprietors' petition was promptly withdrawn.[146]

During this period there were changes also in the person-
nel of the proprietors, which had important consequences to the
landholders in the Northern Neck. Lord Fairfax died January
6, 1709/10.[147] The news seems to have reached Virginia two
months later for Fairfax was recited in the list of proprietors
in two grants dated March 6, 1709/10, after which the books
were closed until July, 1710.[148] Then, and thenceforth until
May, 1711, the proprietors were described as

'Marguritte Lady Culpeper and Catherine Lady Fairfax,
proprietors of the Northern Neck of Virginia.'

Four months after the death of her son-in-law, old Lady
Culpeper died also. She was buried in the Bromfield Chapel
appurtenant to Leeds Castle on May 12, 1710.[149] By a will
dated four days earlier, she had left the greater part of her
individual estate to her grandson, Thomas, now sixth Lord
Fairfax, specifying

'£4,000, which is due me on Mault Tickets, *also my sixth
part of the Virginia Estate.*'

Thus a new proprietor came upon the scene, but for the
moment he was not to be known in Virginia. Being under age
when he thus acquired his first interest in the proprietary, his
grandmother's will was proved by his mother, who also qualified as executrix. In this relation the widowed Lady Fairfax

seems to have lacked the advice of counsel. At all events, she ignored the technical difference between her own title and her guardianship of that of her son. She must have written to Col. Carter that she now combined in her own person the rights of her mother as well as those of her father, for the agent, ignorant of the facts, proceeded to write into the land grants a description of the proprietors which failed to recognise the existence of the new owner of the 'undivided sixth.' Thus was inaugurated, in a grant dated May 9, 1711, to be followed during the remainder of Lady Fairfax's life, the most serious of the several defects in conveyancing with which the Northern Neck grant books bristle. Carrying also another curious, but important, blunder of detail, this description read as follows :[150]

'The Right Honourable Catherine Lady Fairfax, Dutchess Dowager of Cameron in Scotland, the only daughter and heir of Thomas late Lord, and Marguritte late Lady, Culpeper, deceased, sole and only Proprietor of the Northern Neck of Virginia.'

The attribution of Lady Fairfax as 'Dutchess Dowager of Cameron' was, however, immediately corrected to read 'Baroness Dowager.'[151]

1713-1719. *Edmund Jenings and Thomas Lee, agents, N. N., 5.* Land Office 'Mt. Pleasant' in Westmoreland.

The only surviving record of Catherine Culpeper, Lady Fairfax, during her childhood is a portrait with a sedate baby face. She remains silent also as an old fashioned wife during the years she bore and reared her children. She seems to have retired to Leeds Castle at once on her husband's death and thenceforth to have resided there. On the death of her mother she began to reveal herself. Cold by nature, she was, obviously, embittered by the consequences, so costly to her and her children, of her father's irregular domestic relations, and the financial disaster which had overtaken her husband, and

she determined to protect her posterity against a repetition of
such lapses. The motive was admirable, but Lady Fairfax's
manner of expressing it lacked tact. Although she yearned
over her eldest son and signed herself, "your loving mother
till death' in her only letter to him which has survived, she took
a high line with him and maintained it even into her will, trust-
ing him with nothing she could withhold, even after he came
of age in October, 1714. This may be read not only in the
highly coloured family traditions cited by Burnaby, but more
convincingly in the contemporary comment by that downright
old soldier, the contemporary General Thomas Fairfax. Writing from Ireland to Admiral Robert Fairfax in 1710, he said
he hoped 'Lady Fairfax has bowels' enough to do good to her
children.'

She took over the responsibility of the Northern Neck at
a moment when Col. Carter's management was in full swing
of success. Opportunity was knocking at the great oaken door
of the Leeds Castle moat house, but, lacking the business judgment of her mother, Lady Fairfax was not at home to that
particular visitor. After her husband's death she had been
darkly advised by one of her land agents.[152]

'There are some papers of moment relating to the Virginia
estate in the hands of a certain person I know, which will be
of use, and upon an order from your ladyship, I presume he
will deliver them. That Mr. Perry is a sharp man and I fear
you are but very indifferently dealt with by him and his friend
in Virginia and if I don't help you to a chapman for it (which
you shall soon hear further from me about) I doubt not of
putting your ladyship and your lady mother in a way to make
more of it yearly than hath been made since Mr. Perry and his
friend's management thereof.'

On no better evidence than this she decided to remove
Col. Carter from the agency. She turned for advice in her
Virginia affairs from Micajah Perry to Thomas Corbin, an-
other eminent Virginia merchant in London.[153] Corbin's house
had been identified with the Northern Neck for two geenrations.
He nominated as the Virginia resident to take over Carter's

function that tried colonial administrator, his brother-in-law, Edmund Jenings of 'Ripon' in York, who had been both Secretary of State and acting Governor, and had won golden opinions from the Lords of Trade by his discretion in the latter responsibility.[154] Jenings was in England in the autumn of 1711, and though he expected to return to America, his private affairs, which had brought him 'home,' were dragging and it seemed likely, as turned out to be the fact, that he would be delayed. He and Corbin accordingly agreed to put forward as a *locum tenens* a promising young nephew whose name might be expected to appeal to Lady Fairfax, for he was a son of that Richard Lee who had broken the dam of opposition to the proprietary by attorning to her husband. On December 7, 1711, she executed a new procuration revoking that of Robert Carter and constituting as her Northern Neck agent in his stead 'Thomas Lee of the County of Westmoreland in Virga., Merchant.'[155]

The fact that her new resident agent was only three years the senior of her own eldest son, and so had just come of age when his procuration was signed, adds poignancy to the letter, referred to above. This was dated from 'Leeds Castle, December 15, 1711,' or a few days after the date of Lee's power, and in it Lady Fairfax said to her son, then still at Oxford:[156]

'I have done all I can in business in London now, but it is all very bad. Your father hath destroyed all that can be for you and me both: but I will do all that is in my power to get something again, and I do hope you will deserve it of me in time.'

Thomas Lee began his distinguished career, destined to parallel those of Jenings and Carter in relation to the Virginia government as well as the Northern Neck, by taking over the Northern Neck books and establishing on behalf of Lady Fairfax, 'my office in Westmoreland County within my said Proprietary.' This was at his father's house, 'Mt. Pleasant,' on the Potomac.

Lee's power was not as broad as those of the preceding

agents. It was limited in terms to the collection of what was
due the proprietor: nothing was expressed as to executing
grants. The procuration ended, however, with a general clause:

'and generally in and concerning the premises and the de-
pendencys, to do, say, transact and accomplish whatsoever the
said constituant herself might or could doe personally,'

language which, by all rules of interpretation, properly related
only to the previously granted specific authority to collect dues;
but this was assumed to be authority to make grants of lands.
Thereby arose that defect in many Northern Neck land titles
due, as the act of 1736 subsequently recited, to the fact that
the powers contained in Lee's procuration 'were not full and
sufficient to warrant the said agents and attornies to pass away
estates in fee simple.'

On September 1, 1713,[157] Lee opened a new grant book,
and thereafter during three years continued in all respects
Carter's practice in the proprietary office. His single innova-
tion was one for which the student of his records today must
thank him gratefully, namely, that in many instances he recorded maps of the surveys as well as the descriptions of his
grants.

Jenings returned to Virginia in the spring of 1715, and
some months later took over the management of the proprietary. Although the office remained at 'Mt. Pleasant' and
Thomas Lee continued to superintend the books, henceforth,
during the ensuing three years that remained of Lady Fairfax's life, Jenings signed the grants.[158]

Meanwhile Perry and Robert Carter had not been idle.
They were both what the Elizabethans called 'men of their
hands.' Neither accepted cheerfully the affront Lady Fairfax
had put upon them, and they did not fail to obstruct the
Jenings-Lee agency in every way they could. Locally, Carter
stirred up criticism of the conduct of the proprietary office,
which found public expression in the Assembly; but their most
powerful weapon of offense was the plight in which Jenings'
private affairs were involved. He was deeply in debt to Perry,

and Carter inexorably foreclosed a mortgage upon his home place in York County, buying it in for his own account. In his desperation, despite the support of Governor Spotswood, Jenings undoubtedly neglected the affairs of the proprietary; and so Carter was enabled to taste a full measure of revenge when, in 1719, occurred the next demise of the title to the Northern Neck.

During all this period, beginning with the first grant Thomas Lee signed in September, 1713, the conveyancing form Carter had inaugurated in 1703 was continued, even to the mistake in the recital of the proprietors; in that respect, however, the description was simplified to read:

'The Right Honourable Catherine Lady Fairfax, Sole Proprietor of the Northern Neck of Virginia.'

1722-1732. *Robert Carter, agent and lessee. N. N., A.—D. inclusive.*

Land Office 'Corotoman' in Lancaster.

At the end of May, 1719, Lady Fairfax died at Leeds Castle and on June 1st was buried beside her mother in Bromfield Chapel.[159] By her will she devised 'all lands in Virginia' to 'William Cage of Milgate[160] and Edward Filmer of East Sutton[161] . . . in fee on trust,' upon an elaborate entail, providing that the proprietary should be held first by the testatrix's eldest son, Thomas, sixth Lord Fairfax, for life, with remainder to his sons successively in tail male, then over to the testatrix's other sons, and ultimately to her right heirs. Edward Filmer renounced the trust, but William Cage accepted the duty and also qualified as executor. Taking hold of the affairs of the Northern Neck, he apparently consulted Micajah Perry and from him heard the Virginia opinion that Edmund Jenings' conduct of the agency had been a failure, with a suggestion that Robert Carter might again be induced to take charge of the business. There is no surviving record of the ensuing negotiations, but, apparently, Carter stipulated that the only inducement to him would be that he should be vested not only

with the agency but with a lease of the proprietary. For such
a lease he offered a fixed and assured rent of £450 per annum.
This was probably more than had ever been received from
Jenings, and the proprietors closed promptly.[162] Accordingly,
Carter re-opened the proprietary land office at Corotoman with
a grant dated December 1, 1722,[163] in which he inaugurated a
new description of the proprietors, reading as follows:

'The Right Honourable Thomas Lord Fairfax of Leeds
Castle in the County of Kent and Baron of Cameron in Scotland, and William Cage of Millgate in the Parish of Bearstead
in the County of Kent, Esqr., devisee in trust and sole executor
of the last will and testament of the Right Honourable Catherine Lady Fairfax deceased, Proprietors of the Northern Neck
of Virginia.'

The new proprietor had been born at Leeds Castle on
October 22, 1693.[164] Although he was, in consequence, twenty-
five years of age when his mother died, then for the first time
he became a free agent. He celebrated this luxury by seeking a career at the court of George I, where doubtless he
hoped to retrieve the two shattered fortunes to which he had
succeeded. The effort was, however, unsuccessful. When Sir
Robert Walpole came into office Fairfax was swept out of the
one minor post he had achieved. Abandoning then forever all
effort to practice the *art de parvenir,* he retired to the country
to a more congenial life of fox hunting and hound breeding.
He did not even take any active part in the management of the
proprietary. Carter's surviving letters of the time[165] are full of
reproaches that he could get no answer out of the proprietor
on any of the questions the Virginia government was then
raising about his rights. Thus in 1723 he said to the second
Micajah Perry:

'If they do not think fitt to bestirr themselves in the Support of their own Estate I shall have little reason to give my
Self any trouble in throwing myself into the ffrowns of Government. As their Trustee I have done my duty in Hanging
out lights for them.'

Again in 1727, he wrote to Col. Cage:

'If his Lordship will not bestir himself towards the Asserting of his boundaries and defending his Estate I shall have this Satisfaction of having done my duty.'

It thus appears that at this time Fairfax was willing to take what he could get out of his Virginia inheritance and not ask too many questions about it.

Characteristically, Carter was unable to stomach that attitude. He knew the local conditions to be favorable to a profitable development of the proprietary, for the movement of population from tidewater towards the piedmont was now in full flow and he had confidence in his own ability to direct a large part of it to the Northern Neck. Vested with the proprietary rights for his own account, he not only stimulated immigration among the yearly crops of graduating indenture men in the tidewater, and carved out of the piedmont large 'manors' for his children and his friends, but exercised, to the elastic limit of interpretation, all the feudalities which could be deduced from Lord Culpeper's charter of 1688.

Some of these 'regalities' had never been invoked; others had been allowed to lapse during Jenings' agency; when, specifically, the Receiver General was suffered to collect on behalf of the Crown all the deodands and other forfeitures for crime which accrued within the Northern Neck. Carter first asserted a claim to that particular perquisite in 1723, and in due course secured from the Crown law officers an opinion upholding him. His natural arrogance, stimulated by this confirmation of his judgment, then became intolerable to his colleagues in the Council. The important result was the precipitation of the last of the successive attacks by the Virginia government upon the proprietary.[166]

When the incumbents of the Crown patent offices at Williamsburg, who were most interested, Messrs. Grymes and Blair (the Receiver General and the Deputy Auditor) realized that Carter's activities were steadily diminishing their commissions, they determined, in the interest of their offices, to confine the proprietary within the straitest possible limits. To that end they revived the controversy about the bounds of the Northern Neck, which had been dormant since 1706. The Council Journal shows that the question came up on June 11, 1729, when Col. Carter was present, and it was agreed that a case should be made up of the points at issue, for mutual submission to the Crown. Carter seems at once to have certified this proposal to his principal, with a suggestion that compromise was expedient. He received in reply no more satisfaction than a statement that under the entail created by his mother's will the proprietor had no power to alienate any of the proprietary rights, and that compromise of the boundaries necessarily involved alienation. One can imagine that this answer must have aggravated Col. Carter's tendency to apoplexy. At all events, he now threw up his hands and, after waiting a year, the Virginia government proceeded to force the issue for its own account.

In June, 1730, the Assemly adopted that able petition to the Crown against 'the Exorbitant and Unwarrantable powers' contained in the Northern Neck patent, which John Clayton formulated.[167] This petition was at once sent to England but was lost at sea, so that the duplicate, subsequently sent home, did not reach the Privy Council until after Robert Carter was dead.

Micajah Perry had already preceded him to the grave, and a new generation was soon to be in the saddle.

1734-1747. *William Fairfax, agent. N. N., E-F, inclusive.*
Land Offices, Nomini in Westmoreland, 1736-1737.
　　　　　　　Falmouth in King George, 1737-1741.
　　　　　　　Belvoir in Prince William (after 1742, Fairfax), 1741-1747.

In the summer of 1732 the proprietor was surprised by the necessity for two vital decisions, the appointment of a new resident agent in Virginia, and the resistance of a carefully planned attack upon his patrimony. Roused by the crisis, he now at last took vigorous action. In July, 1733, he retorted upon the Assembly by himself also filing a petition to the Crown, which recited the persistent encroachments by the Virginia government and prayed a judicial ascertainment of the boundaries of his proprietary.[168] A few weeks later, on August 26th, the Commissioners of the Customs ordered that 'William Fairfax, now Collector of Salem, be removed to be Collector of South Potomac river, Virginia, if the office be found on inquiry to be vacant;[169] on February 21, 1733/4, Lord Fairfax executed a special power of attorney in respect of his affairs in Virginia, to 'William Fairfax, Esq., Collector of the Customs of the River Potomack in Virginia;'[170] and, on June 18, 1734, armed with this authority, the new agent sailed from Salem, bound for his new post.[171]

On his arrival in the Potomac William Fairfax took up a temporary residence in the Nomini neighbourhood of Westmoreland, where he found the South Potomac custom house established, and accordingly it was in Westmoreland Court that he took his oath in relation to the customs on August 27, 1734.[172] On the September 5th following, he was included in the commission of the peace for that county.[173]

In May, 1735, the Proprietor himself first set foot in Virginia. He came out on a man-of-war, armed with letters of introduction to Governor Gooch from the Duke of Newcastle and other official potentates, and, after visits of ceremony in Williamsburg, went to stop with his kinsman in Westmoreland.[174] Thence were conducted the preliminaries of the negotiations with the Virginia government which had brought Lord Fairfax across the ocean.

These negotiations opened auspiciously. Their first fruits were garnered at the next ensuing session of the Assembly, when, with Fairfax's acquiescence, there was enacted, on September 23, 1736,[175] the

'Act for confirming and better securing the titles to lands in the Northern Neck, held under the Right Honourable Thomas Lord Fairfax, Baron of Cameron in that part of Great Britain called Scotland.'

Fairfax had come out rather as an ambassador for his family than as a claimant that he was himself vested with the full proprietary title. He well knew that he held in his own right only an undivided one-sixth; that of the other five-sixths he was no more than the beneficiary for life under the trust created by his mother's will, not even the tenant in tail in the strict legal meaning of the term. In this situation, on the advice of counsel in England, Fairfax had instructed Robert Carter that he and his trustee had no power to continue the kind of grants which had always been customary in the Northern Neck, and thus had thrown doubt on all the titles Carter created during the term of his second agency. Everyone seemed now to recognise that the complication presented by such an interpretation of Catherine Culpeper's will was intolerable. So far as concerned Virginia, the seating of a fourth of the colony could not be arrested because an embittered woman had been suspicious that her eldest son might prove as extravagant as his father; and that son was himself unwilling longer to be held in tutelage. The problem was to find a way out. Apparently the astute Edward Barradall, who was now advising Fairfax locally, became the Alexander who cut the Gordian knot by drafting the act to which reference has been made.

The bill was introduced by Edwin Conway of Lancaster on September 13, 1736. Within ten days, during which Fairfax was the guest of Governor Gooch at 'the Palace' and there publicly expressed his agreement, it went through all the processes of legislation, including the necessary assent by the Governor.

After reciting at length the Northern Neck charters of 1669 and 1688, this act proceeded:

'*Whereas* the right honourable Thomas Lord Fairfax baron of Cameron in that part of Great Britain called Scotland, heir at law to the said Thomas Lord Culpeper, is now become Sole proprietor of the said territory with the appurtenances and the above recited letters patents and

'*Whereas* divers great quantities of land have been granted to adventurers and planters within the said territory in fee simple by the agents and attornies of the said Lord Fairfax and his predecessors, former proprieters of the said territory, under letters patents, by virtue of divers letters of attorney from time to time by them respectively given and granted to their said attornies and agents: but now of late, after long possessions, and great and valuable improvements made upon the said lands by such grantees, questions are like to arise between them and the said proprietor touching the validity of such grants, as well in respect to a construction set up and maintained of the said letters of attorney, that the powers therein contained were not full and sufficient to enable and warrant the said agents and attornies to pass away estates in fee simple, as in respect of the said lord proprietors estate in the premises, the same being now held by him as tenant in tail under the will or wills of some of his ancestors: whereby the minds of many of his majesty's good subjects, possessors of lands and tenements within the said territory are greatly disquieted and many controversies and expensive law suits may probably ensue: For the prevention whereof and for settling peace between his lordship and his said tenants

'*Be it enacted, etc.,* That from henceforth all and every grant and grants heretofore duly and regularly made and passed by the agents or attornies of the proprietors of the said territory, or any of them, shall be good available and binding in law, to pass such estate or estates as therein have been granted; and the grantees their heirs and assigns respectively shall forever hereafter peaceably and quietly have hold and enjoy the same granted premises according to such granted estates, under the rents and services by the said grants reserved, notwithstanding the infancy, coverture, or any misprision or mistake of the names, dignity or title of the said proprietors or either of them; or any misrecital, omission or defect in the said grant or grants, or any of them: so as the same have been made and signed by the agents or attornies of the said proprietors or the husband, guardian or guardians, trustee or trustees, of any of them and passed under the common seal of office kept by them for that purpose.

This interesting legislation was in effect a treaty between the colony and the proprietor, superseding, as only a treaty might, all other rules of law. Its provision was that in consideration of the waiver of the many cumulative conveyancing irregularities by the successive agents, and the ratification by the proprietor of all grants previously made by them, Virginia recognised Fairfax as sole owner of the fee. There was discreet silence on both sides as to the powers of either in the premises.

After the act had been duly ratified by the Crown, as it was on May 25, 1738,[176] no question of the terms of Lady Fairfax's will was ever again raised. Her trustee forthwith dropped out of the record and the remainder men kept silence. They were satisfied by a family compact under which Lord Fairfax subsequently made over Leeds Castle and the other Culpeper estates in Kent to his brother Robert, to be held by him in tail and agreed that after his own death his mother's interest in the proprietary should revert as part of the same inheritance. If there is any surviving record of that compact among the muniments of the present owners of Leeds Castle, it is not available to the historian, who must be content with the tradition quoted by Burnaby and the confirmatory testimony recorded by Lord Fairfax himself in his will, written nearly half a century later. There he set down a recognition of persisting differences in the terms of his tenure of the historical one-sixth and five-sixths of the proprietary. This was destined to puzzle the Virginia courts, for their record, based on the act of 1736, lacked the wills of Lady Culpeper and her daughter; but, fortunately for the thousands who were then in possession of Northern Neck lands under titles derived from Lord Fairfax individually, there were no new complications on that account. By the time of the final judicial review of the proprietary title in relation to the rights of individual grantees, all such questions which had not been barred by time had been cured by that most effective silencer of the law—Revolution.[177]

After Lord Fairfax and Governor Gooch had agreed upon the principles of the act of 1736, it seems that it must have been suggested that when the Assembly met, which was to consider that legislation, a good impression of Lord Fairfax's declared plans would be created, if it could be announced that the Northern Neck land office had been reopened and that those who had been waiting ever since Robert Carter's death could now currently procure grants. At all events, the records show that on July 21, 1736, Lord Fairfax signed a grant,[178] reciting it to have been 'Given at my office in Westmoreland County.'

This office was evidently at the custom house at Nomini, but it was not long maintained there, for in the spring of 1737 William Fairfax removed his residence from the Potomac to the Rappahannock and established himself in a rented house near Falmouth in King George. Thenceforth, beginning with one dated June 6, 1737, the grants were 'Given at my office in the county of King George.'[179]

All the grants issued during this year (July, 1736-September, 1737) were signed by Lord Fairfax himself. In form they perpetuated *totidem verbis* the precedent Robert Carter had established in 1703, except that, adopting the principle of the act of 1736, the description of the proprietor now read:

'The Right Honourable Thomas Lord Fairfax, Baron of Cameron in that part of Great Britain called Scotland, Proprietor of the Northern Neck of Virginia.'

In that form and by that description all grants were thenceforth issued until the Northern Neck books were finally closed by the proprietor's death at the end of 1781.

After the passage of the act of 1736 Lord Fairfax remained in Virginia to carry through the survey of the proprietary, which in response to his petition had been directed by an Order of Council of November 29, 1733. While the survey was in progress he rode over the proprietary and, from what he saw, carved out for his own individual development the two manors thenceforth known as 'Leeds' and 'Great Falls.' These reservations and the implications of the family settlement based on the act of 1736, as well as his conversations with the Virginians he met, indicate that Fairfax looked forward to spending a part of his time in America, if he had not yet determined to reside there.[180] His immediate obligation was, however, to gain his suit with the Virginia government and establish his bounds beyond peradventure. The animus developed by the survey showed how much there was at stake, either to

gain or to lose. Accordingly, in September, 1737, Fairfax
'very privately embarked in Rappahannock River in the very
last ship bound from thence for London.'[181]

What was of concern to Virginia in this departure was
that the Northern Neck land office thereupon closed again. Like
all litigants, Fairfax may well have expected a prompt adjudication, enabling him to return once more to Virginia to put
the proprietary office on a permanent footing before the sus-
pension of grants had caused further serious inconvenience. Before he left he had signed grants in all pressing cases and so
did not deem it necessary to leave with William Fairfax any
power to issue more. The new agent's procuration of 1734
was, indeed, merely a warrant to collect quit rents; it made no
mention of grants at all.

But when the proprietor reached England he faced a long
prospect of the law's delays. William Byrd's lively record of
the survey provides the clue in a tart observation that 'having
formerly withstood the Ministry in the election for the County
of Kent his Affair moved very heavily.' In resentment of Sir
Robert Walpole's ancient slight upon him, Fairfax had given
his support to the 'patriot' faction of the day, that 'country
party' to which Squire Western also belonged, and so was out
of favor at George II's court. Although he diligently pressed
his suit in person before the Lords of Trade, of whom the
Privy Council had asked a report, he soon found that he could
not expect to return to Virginia for several years. It was then
he decided to enlarge the powers of his agent so that the Northern Neck office might again be opened. William Fairfax's
new procuration was dated January 24, 1738/9,[182] and gave
him specific power

'to grant to any person or persons of ability any part of
the lands tenements or hereditaments heretofore and now in the
possession of or anyways belonging to me the said Thomas,
Lord Fairfax, in Virginia, in such manner and for such considerations as to my said attorney shall seem fitting, and grants
thereof in due form in my name to execute.'

Under this authority the agent re-opened the land office in May, 1739, and began to issue grants in his own discretion as Robert Carter and the other resident agents previously had done. All these grants, like those executed in 1737 by the proprietor himself, were 'Given at my Office in the County of King George,' until October, 1741, when the equivalent recital was changed to read 'in the County of Prince William.' It was then that William Fairfax removed his residence and the proprietary office from Falmouth to Belvoir on the Potomac.[183]

Meanwhile Lord Fairfax had at last gained his cause. After the Walpole administration fell, the sky cleared for him. That he then wrote to his friends in Virginia in high spirits, predicting an early victory and his return to America, appears from a surviving reply:

'Sir R. Walpole and his party,' said William Beverley of Blandfield on August 9, 1742,[184] 'have had a long reign of it, to the great prejudice of the Kingdom; and now the Country party have prevailed, I hope the affairs will soon take another turn; tho' as your Lordship observes it will not be pleasing to some of our gentry here. As your friends are now in play, I hope you will have justice done you without delay.'

Fairfax still played his cards cautiously, taking no chances. One evidence of this is that he retained that celebrated advocate, William Murray (later Lord Mansfield and Chief Justice), who was *persona gratissima* to the 'broad bottom' ministry. It was by Murray's adroit management that, a month after Walpole's death, there was at last secured an Order in Council which was worth all the delay and anxiety of the seven years since the Proprietor had left Virginia.

This decree of April 11, 1745,[185] began by reciting the report of the Lords of Trade setting forth elaborately a review of the facts in controversy, based on the rival reports and maps submitted by the Commissioners for Virginia and Fairfax, respectively, and then adjudged:

'His Majesty this day took the said Report into Consideration, and was pleased, with the advice of His Privy Council to

Approve thereof, and to Declare and Order as it is hereby
Declared and Ordered, that within the words and meaning of
the Letters Patent granted by King James the Second, bearing
date the 27th day of September in the Fourth Year of his
Reign, the Boundary of the Petitioners Land doth begin at
the first Spring of the South Branch of the River Rappahannock now called Rappidan, which first Spring is the Spring
of that part of the said River called Rappidan as is called in
the Plans returned, by the name of Conway River, And that
the said Boundary be from thence drawn in a Strait Line North
West to the place in the Alagany Mountains where that part of
the River Patawomeck alias Potowmack which is now called
Cohongoroota alias Cohongoronton first arises; the other
Boundarys being the said Rivers themselves as they run from
their said respective Heads till they fall into Chesapeyock alias
Chesapeak Bay. . . .

'And that the said Governor or Commander in Chief do
not make any Grants of Lands within the said Boundarys, nor
Molest or Disturb the Petitioner in the quiet possession and
Enjoyment of the Lands contained therein, but the said Lands
to be Subject to the Grants made of any parts thereof by His
Majesty or any of his Royal Predecessors, and so as the said
Lord Fairfax do Comply with his proposal mentioned in the
aforegoing Report.

'And His Majesty doth hereby likewise Signify His Royal
Pleasure, that the Lord Fairfax shall for the future be intitled
to all the Advantages Profits and Emoluments whatsoever to
arise from Grants, made by the Crown, of Lands within his
Boundarys, which the Crown would or might have been intitled
to by the Terms, or in consequence of the said Grants; and
where, upon such Grants, Quit Rents are reserved, that he the
said Lord Fairfax shall be intitled to demand and receive the
same from the Grantees to his own use and benefit from the
time that this Order shall be made known to the said Governor and to his Majestys Receiver General of the Quit Rents
in that Province.'

It will be noted that this decree completely justified Robert
Carter's interpretation of the charter of 1688. Practically, its
immediate effect was to require Virginia to surrender to the
Proprietor all the lands which had been in dispute since 1706,
subject only to Lord Fairfax's volunteered stipulation to the
Lords of Trade to confirm the titles of all 'grantees of Lands

under the Crown.'[186] This included both the Great Fork of the Rappahannock, which had been seated as part of Orange and was now to become the county of Culpeper, and the newer settlements beyond the Blue Ridge, which had recently been set up as the county of Frederick. But more than that, looking to the future, it put into Fairfax's hands the development of a vast western frontier which in 1745 was still an unseated wilderness.

It remained to survey and map the western boundary of the proprietary, and that was accomplished in the summer of 1746 by commissioners appointed respectively by the Virginia government and the proprietor. Another chapter of Northern Neck history closed with the planting of 'Fairfax Stones' at the head spring of the Potomac on October 23, and at the head spring of Conway on November 13, 1746.[187]

1747-1781. *George William Fairfax, agent, 1747-1762, N. N., F-I.*
Thomas Bryan Martin, agent, 1762-1781, N. N., I-S.
Land offices:
    'Belvoir' in Fairfax, 1747-1762.
    'Greenway Court' in Frederick, 1762-1781.

By the spring of 1747, the proprietor had disposed of every detail of his protracted litigation, and had made effective the family compact already referred to. He had seen his younger brother, Robert, established in possession of Leeds Castle, married, and elected to Parliament, and had himself performed the characteristic English duty, almost equivalent to making a will, of having his portrait painted. So, at the age of 53, he was free to retire from the great world in which fortune had sorely buffeted him. He accordingly decided to return to Virginia.

At the same time William Fairfax, two years his cousin's senior, was preparing to lay down some of his responsibilities also. During the absence of the proprietor he had achieved fortune and the highest colonial dignity. He had become a large landholder not only at Belvoir but elsewhere in the pro-

prietary, principally below the Shenandoah at its mouth, and
a member of 'His Majesty's Council of State.' He appreciated that with the return of the Proprietor the duty of the
Northern Neck agency was destined to become no more than
supervision of the office, and he settled back upon the easy
and comfortable function of Collector of Customs for South
Potomac as his chief remaining activity. In this situation the
turn of his life was emphasized by three recent events in his
family, the loss of his wife and a beloved younger son (the
latter killed in action in the navy), and the arrival in Virginia
of his promising eldest son, just of age, and fresh from the
English education for which he had been sent from Salem
sixteen years before.

For all these considerations William Fairfax proposed to
the proprietor to surrender the Northern Neck agency with
its 'salary of two or three hundred [pounds] a year'[188] to George
William Fairfax and so set him up in life at once on his arrival
in Virginia. Lord Fairfax sent for the young man out of
Yorkshire to visit him at Leeds Castle in order to look him
over. He found him not only a sympathetic sportsman in the
hunting field, but already a man of character, and he gave him
at once his confidence and affection.[189]

Arriving in the Potomac in May, 1747,[190] with the purpose of establishing a residence somewhere in his new manor
of Leeds, the proprietor went to Belvoir, and there began once
more himself to sign Northern Neck grants, as thenceforth he
continued to do for nearly half a century.[191] For this reason
the Grant Books no longer provide certain evidence of changes
in the agency; but it seems reasonably certain that in the autumn
of 1747, George Fairfax was put in charge of the Northern
Neck office at Belvoir. This would explain how he came to
be in charge of the expedition to subdivide the proprietor's
South Branch manor in the following March;[192] but, whether
it was then or some months later, before October, 1751, certainly, William Fairfax had laid down the responsibility, and
his son was exercising it.[193]

In this relation the land office remained at Belvoir until

January 1, 1762, when it was transferred to Greenway Court in Frederick.

Lord Fairfax testified that in July, 1749, he opened a branch land office in Frederick 'for the county.'[194] This seems to have been the time when the proprietor established that residence in Frederick which Capt. Dalrymple depicted on the 1755 edition of the Fry and Jefferson map. The reference to this site as 'his Lordships Quarter' in March, 1747/8,[195] indicates that, though seated that early, it was not yet a place of residence; but when to the date of opening the branch office is added the record that, in October, 1749, Lord Fairfax was commissioned a justice of the peace in all the counties of the proprietary, it is persuasive that coincidentally with his assumption of the responsibilities of resident citizenship he settled down in his Frederick 'quarter.'[196]

At all events, the proprietor was living beyond the Blue Ridge in the summer of 1751, when his young nephew, Thomas Bryan Martin, came out to Virginia to make a career, and after a visit at Belvoir joined his uncle in Frederick. He so endeared himself that on May 21, 1752, when he came of age, 'in consideration of the natural affection I have and bear unto the said Thomas Bryan Martin as my Nephew,' the proprietor granted to him 8,840 acres lying west of Leeds manor and beyond the Shenandoah, 'to be known and call'd by the Name of the Manor of Greenway Court.'[197] This was the land on which the Proprietor was then living.

When it became apparent that Lord Fairfax was indefinitely postponing his plans to build the manor house on a western spur of the Blue Ridge, for which he had brought furniture and other equipment from England, Martin repeatedly urged that the office should be under the proprietor's own eye. The delays and inconvenience of sending papers back and forth between Greenway Court and Belvoir was obvious, and it was also a fact that, most of the lands below the Blue Ridge having been granted away, the current activities of the office were now chiefly concerned with the lands of the transmontane counties of Frederick and Hampshire. But Lord Fairfax was steadfast in his affection for his young cousin George and until the latter went to England in 1760 to take possession of his Yorkshire estate there was apparently no serious question of effecting such a move.

Writing to the proprietor from Belvoir on May 1, 1760, George Fairfax outlined his plans for carrying on the business during his absence, in a letter which gives a picture of the office at that time:[198]

'I shall be glad to know whether you have thought of any person to keep the Office and how the books are to be disposed of; for I am afraid I can't accomplish my trip under twelve or eighteen months in which time the business might suffer. Mr. Carlyle [of Alexandria, his brother-in-law] has informed me that you signified a desire of removing down, which I wish could be convenient, and then the same hand now in the office, and under your Eye and direction could continue the business; but if that be not agreeable and you have no person in view I will endeavor to leave things in the best situation I can, and I am certain Mr. Dent [the clerk of the office] is so well qualified now that he can do and keep all the ordinary business; and if you have a mind the several receivers may be directed to make their returns of money to you, or any person you may please to direct. The Rev. Mr. Green [parson of Truro] has kindly offered you or me any service in his power, and I think when there is any intricate affair, I don't know of any that I would sooner accept, for he has been formerly well acquainted with the office business, and is able to examine any plot that can be brought before him. Or I dare say Col. Washington would inspect into these affairs during my absence. But these methods I only mention in case you have not fixed upon any one for these purposes, for I am far from desiring the continuance of the business, but would willingly do all in my power to increase your revenue. I am getting things ready to repair the house and if your Lordship is inclined, I will endeavor to make it as agreeable as possible, and truly say you shall be heartily welcome.'

Two months later this was followed by a formal application 'more particularly obtaining your permission of absence for a few years about some private affairs of great consequence to myself and family.' George Fairfax remained in

England on this occasion for nearly three years, and that absence accomplished what neither argument nor blandishments could do. Writing to George Washington from Yorkshire under date of October 30, 1761, he said:[199]

'I am informed by many hands, tho' not from the performers, that an Office is really building at Greenway Court. . . . It gives me the most concern to find what an influence Martin has.'

Again, in September, 1762, he wrote to Major Robert Fairfax at Leeds Castle:[200]

'Mr. M. has carried his long laboured point of getting the management of the Office into his own hands, and removing it with them to Frederick.'

The land books confirm this, for, beginning with January 1, 1762, and thenceforth until April, 1780, the grants all recited that they were 'Given at my Office in the County of Frederick.'[201]

1782-1786. Bryan Fairfax, agent.

When Cornwallis surrendered at Yorktown, the proprietor was still at Greenway Court, but bent under the infirmities of age. He was then in his eighty-ninth year. For more than a year he had been unable to sign grants or otherwise attend to business; but Bryan Martin had continued to issue warrants for new surveys. In this situation, on December 9, 1781, Lord Fairfax died. His interest in the proprietary then resolved itself into its component parts. The five-sixths thereof which Catherine Culpeper had inherited from her father, and which, despite the local interpretation of the colonial act of 1736, her children had continued to regard as bound by the entail of her will, devolved under the terms of that will upon the late proprietor's younger brother, Robert Fairfax of Leeds Castle, who now succeeded as seventh Lord Fairfax;[202] but the undivided sixth which had originally belonged to Alexander Culpeper and had been by him devised to Margaret, Lady Culpeper and by her to her eldest grandson, together with all the manors which the late proprietor had carved out of the Northern Neck and of which he died seized in fee simple, were devised by his will to the eldest surviving son of his sister, Frances, widow of Denny Martin of Salt Place in Loose, co. Kent.[203]

As on the occasion of all previous devolutions of the proprietary title, the Northern Neck land office was closed immediately on the sixth Lord Fairfax's death; but in this instance, departing from precedent, it was never opened again in the name of a proprietor. Anticipating his brother's end, Robert Fairfax had given to George Fairfax a procuration to resume the proprietary agency, and in the spring of 1782, on receipt of news of the demise, the latter deputed his brother, Bryan Fairfax, to act for him.[204] When Bryan Fairfax made demand upon Bryan Martin for possession of the office the latter opposed difficulties, so that on May 9, 1783, Robert, Lord Fairfax, wrote to Bryan Fairfax, transmitting a new power of attorney[205] and adding:

'Doctor Martin (now taken the name of Fairfax) having consented that my Agent shall conduct and do the whole business of the Proprietary, has also sent a power of attorney to his Brother [to receive from Bryan Fairfax his 'just fair nett sixth part,' and] directing him to deliver up all the official papers.'

But before Bryan Fairfax could act upon this authority, the revolutionary Virginia Assembly, by a contemporary act (October session, 1782), reciting that 'there is reason to suppose the said proprietorship hath descended upon alien enemies,' sequestered the Northern Neck quit rents as the first step of progressive proceedings which lead to the definite extinction of the charter which Lord Culpeper had left as an inheritance for his descendants.[206] Thus remitted to a mere claim, Bryan Fairfax retained Edmund Randolph and, after the Jay treaty had been ratified with its assurance of protection of alien titles to lands in America, filed with the Assembly a memorial on behalf of the proprietors, praying either a restoration of the quit rents or compensation in the premises. On April 15, 1786, he reported to Robert, Lord Fairfax the futile result of these proposals:

'Having waited some time for an authentic Account of the Event of a memorial which I had presented to the Assembly the last Session, I now write to inform yr Lordship that I can't learn that it had any good Effect. It was received and referred, but the Quit rents are abolished, and as to any Compensation that may or may not be granted at a future day,—It seems to be very uncertain whether any will be ever given. . . . I have been much concerned about this Business, but I have the Satisfaction to think that I have done as much as I would have done for myself.'

Upon this report Lord Fairfax abandoned hope of relief from Virginia and devoted his energies to prosecuting a claim against the English government for compensation of his loss under the provisions of the act of Parliament relating to American Loyalist claims.[207] Bryan Fairfax's agency thus came to an end in inanition.

Meanwhile, in 1784, Denny Martin had come out to Virginia to look after his own interests and, consulting that rising young lawyer John Marshall, was advised to make a fight under the provisions of the Jay Treaty to the end that Virginia might at least be forced to a compromise. Martin accordingly precipitated a litigation which was to keep the courts busy for many years.

In this situation Robert, Lord Fairfax, died and Martin succeeded, under the entail of Catherine Culpeper's will, to the remainder of the proprietary claims which had not been vested in him by the will of the sixth Lord Fairfax. For all that this seemed to strengthen his hand, Martin, being no longer young and appalled by the prospect of lawyers' fees without immediate income, soon acknowledged himself *de guerre lasse*. His alert counsel, confident of success, thereupon took advantage of what seemed a glittering opportunity. On behalf of a

syndicate, which was to be financed by Robert Morris of Phila-
delphia, Marshall made Martin an offer to buy for £20,000 all
his rights arising out of the proprietary, and a bargain was
struck on May 17, 1793. As it turned out, Marshall's confidence in the strategy of his position was justified. Although
he did not complete the stipulated payments until 1806 and it
remained for the youngest and last survivor of the Martin
brothers to make the final deed, in 1796 Marshall effected his
contemplated settlement with the Commonwealth, whereby his
syndicate was assured of the title to Lord Fairfax's 'manors'
in consideration of a waiver of the proprietary jurisdiction.[208]

In relation to the present study this treaty is of significance
in that it gave colour of legality to the destruction of the proprietary as a going concern. Practically, however, there had
been no vitality in it since 1785, when the Assembly directed
'the executive' to remove the proprietary grant books from
Greenway Court and to deposit them as public records in the
Land Office at Richmond. At the same time the Governor
was authorized to make grants in the name of the Commonwealth, confirming all entries made during the life of the late
proprietor for which unsatisfied proprietary warrants were still
outstanding. To that end a special form of grant was used,
the recitals of which were, *e. g.*, as follows:

[The Commonwealth Form]

'*Patrick Henry, Esquire*, Governor of the Commonwealth of Vir-
ginia, to all to whom these presents shall come, Greeting.
'*Know Ye* that by virtue of a warrant from the Lord Proprietor's
Office in the Northern Neck of Virginia, there is granted by the said
Commonwealth unto Martin Pickett . . . '

This was the final official recognition of the Northern
Neck proprietary as an institution, but its shadow was destined
to lengthen for nearly three quarters of a century to come.
Although uniformity of practice throughout the Commonwealth was achieved in 1785 by extending the general land
law to the Northern Neck so that 'waste' lands which were

covered neither by proprietary warrants nor surveys might be taken up through the agency of the county surveyors and the Register of the Land Office, the historical boundary of the Rappahannock was still respected, as under similar circumstances that of the river Trent had been in England. The evidence of this persistence of tradition was that, until 1862, all Commonwealth grants for Northern Neck lands were recorded in the same special series of Grant Books which Philip Ludwell had inaugurated in 1690.[209]

CHAPTER THREE

*The Original difference and Ultimate accord between the
Land Patent and the Northern Neck Grant.*

NO student of the political records of Virginia has failed
to note, often with surprise, the sudden change of local
sentiment with respect to the Northern Neck proprietary
after the close of the seventeenth century. About 1705 the
descendants of those who had seated plantations above the Rappahannock under Virginia patents and had vigorously protested
the existence of the proprietary, peacefully paid their quit rents
to the proprietors: and, without change of its terms or conveyancing forms, the proprietary land office became, under Robert Carter, a freely flowing source of grants of hitherto 'waste'
lands. The standard explanation of this *volteface* is Beverley's,
that the example of the second Richard Lee induced his neighbours to attorn to the proprietors. Other historians have put
the emphasis on the exercise on their behalf of Robert Carter's
dominant influence in the colony. These individual local forces
were clearly important in accomplishing the healing of old sores.
They supplemented medicinally the slow attrition upon the
Northern Neck planters of the persistent support which the
English government gave the proprietors at home. But potent
as were these forces in preparation for the long era of good
feeling during which the last proprietor lived at Greenway
Court, there were other and fundamental considerations for
the ultimate popular acceptance of the proprietary as an institution. The evidence for these forces of peace has been arrayed in the foregoing chapters: it is proposed here to attempt
a generalization from that evidence in aid of an answer to a
challenging historical question.

The original objection to the establishment of proprietors
in Virginia was undoubtedly based less upon the always diffi-

cult relation between a tenant and an absentee landlord than upon the not unreasonable expectation that such gentry would, if they could, collect quit rents, fines and forfeitures, and enforce escheats much more consistently than experience had shown the Crown likely to do.[210] The fact was, indeed, that between the dissolution of the Virginia Company (1624) and the appointment of William Blathwayt as Auditor General for America (1680) the Virginia quit rents were so negligently collected that during Berkeley's second administration, when the question of proprietors was flagrant, the colony began to feel that direct dependence upon the Crown was almost an assurance of immunity in respect to such charges. The vigorous proceedings by Blathwayt after the Crown had resumed the Arlington grant served to dispel this illusion and, incidentally, wiped out any practical advantage in holding land of the Crown as compared with holding of the proprietors of the Northern Neck.[211]

Thus it came about that when Lord Fairfax first came out to Virginia and made his treaty with the colony (1736) the original animosity against proprietors in Virginia in so far as it consisted in a contrast of advantage in the matter of immunity from the strict obligation of quit rents above and below the Rappahannock, had long lost its fire. Indeed, the shoe was upon the other foot, for throughout the period from the death of Lord Culpeper (1688) until the death of his grandson (1781), when the Virginia government was active in enforcing the quit rents in its territory, it was only during Robert Carter's lease of the proprietary (1722-1731) that the quit rent collectors in the Northern Neck were similarly insistent upon the full measure of their pound of flesh. As compared with Williamsburg, Lord Fairfax was an 'easy boss.'[212]

A more subtle, but none the less effective, influence on behalf of the proprietors was the accord accomplished between the conveyancing practice of the government land office and their own. This was a fruit of the decay of the head right as an institution due to self abuse in the exercise of that privilege by the Virginians.

There was never any substantial difference between the titles created by the Virginia land patent and the Northern Neck grant. Both were founded on the seventeenth century development of the feudal law of the manor. The Virginia Company took its estate as part of the royal manor of East Greenwich, and the proprietors took theirs as of a new manor created for their benefit. In this relation the Company and the proprietors were both tenants in capite, holding of the Crown by that most esteemed of all English estates of inheritance 'free and common socage.' Although legally they might have conveyed a title of less dignity (and, indeed, the Company tried to do so), in practice both transferred to their grantees the same title they took. The dissolution of the Company does not modify this parallel, for that action did not promote the individual planter to the feudal status which the Company had had. When the proprietors opened their land office in 1690 the planter who was seated under a grant by the Virginia government was still a manorial tenant. He now held of the King, but as lord of the manor of East Greenwich, not as sovereign. He was, indeel, technically a tenant in capite, but he held, in the language of the old law, *ut de honore,* not, like his predecessor the Company and the proprietors, *ut de corona.* His immediate relation to the Crown thus gave him no more practical rights in respect to his land, and no other advantage, either economic, or social, than could be claimed and exercised by those of his fellows who elected to take Northern Neck grants. The title was uniformly called a fee simple in both jurisdictions, as much in the Northern Neck, where the modern 'republican' historian paints his romantic picture of the attempt of the proprietors to degrade the planter into a serf, as below the Rappahannock.

The substantial difference of conveyancing practice in the two jurisdictions during the generation of controversy was in respect to the consideration moving to a grant.

It had been shown that the gravamen of the persistent demand from Virginia, during the generation following the

Restoration, that the Crown resume the Northern Neck charter was not that private rights had been thereby disregarded, but that the colony was entitled to seat the territory on the terms which had been laid down by the Company when the Northern Neck was under its technical jurisdiction. The answer made to this claim by the proprietors was that the Company had never reduced the Northern Neck to possession and that the seatings which had planted it were made after notice of the charter of 1649. All this was, of course, highly technical on both sides. On the merits it seems likely that if the 'head right,' which was displayed as the badge of the colony's claim, had been practised in 1660 and in 1690, as it was in 1625, Virginia would undoubtedly have been in a stronger position to accomplish her end.

The head right had been progressively degraded throughout the seventeenth century. In the days of the Company everyone who came to Virginia at his own cost became a member of the Company by virtue of immigration, and in that right was entitled to his 'dividend' of fifty acres. After the Restoration the status of what may be called the statistical immigrant was less dignified. There was no longer any Company in which he might be enrolled, while the proportion of individuals who paid their own passage had so materially decreased that in the great majority of cases he was now an indentured servant if he was not a negro slave. Such immigrants neither became landholders on their arrival, nor were they allowed to reserve for future exercise the head rights they created. What had been a 'dividend' came in consequence to be called an 'importation right,' connoting that it had degenerated into the negotiable warrant on which was based an extensive speculation. It was the currency of a trade between the sea captain who claimed the 'rights' of his servant passenger, and the planter who exercised them in the land office.

In the face of these conditions the proprietors went far to meet local expectations. An intelligent foreigner comparing their nominal powers with their practice, without knowledge of their difficulties, might, indeed, have been astonished at their moderation. When they succeeded in establishing their land office in 1690, they gave notice that their 'waste' lands were open to seating to all actual settlers on terms strictly within the local precedents. They offered to convey the same technical estate of inheritance to which Virginians were accustomed. Disregarding Lord Baltimore's example of charging a quit rent of four shillings a hundred acres, they acquiesced in the Virginia quit rent at half that rate. But in lieu of the head right they proposed the alternative established by the Virginia Company of the so-called 'treasury right,' i. e., they stipulated that the planter should pay a 'composition' for the privilege of entry for new lands. Their answer to the objection that this was potentially oppressive was eminently practical; they limited their composition, as they did their quit rent, to a uniform nominal rate; in this case to a figure far less than either the unit of adventure in the Virginia Company (£12, 10s.), the actual cost of importation of an individual, or the productive value of the lands granted. There was no attempt to establish a rack rent basis.

It was, nevertheless, these proposals which the Assembly denounced in 1695 as 'strange and exorbitant practices now used by the honourable L'ds agents.' In considering this language it should be remembered that when it was uttered all the fundamental objections to the proprietary which had stirred the colony in 1667 and 1675, had been met. The emphasis given to this late protest by sending it as an Address to the Crown seems, then, to be evidence not that the current proceedings of the proprietors were necessarily unreasonable, but rather that those who inspired the action of the Assembly were interested in promoting the head right speculation, to which the proprietors refused to submit their lands. At all events, the fervor of the historian's moral indignation against the proprietors' rapacity and selfish disregard of the rights of the poor but honest planters of the Northern Neck must cool when he examines the specifications by the Assembly of their charges.

Assuming that nothing was held back, that the worst that

could be proved against the proprietors in 1695 was alleged, here in seven heads is the sum total of their iniquity, viz:

1.   *They 'demand double the rent the King accepted.'*

This indicates no more than that Messrs. Brent and Fitzhugh had made an attempt in 1694 to introduce into the Northern Neck the Maryland practice of charging a quit rent of four shillings per hundred acres.   But whatever they 'demanded,' their grant books show that in only one insignificant case (*N. N.,* 2: 143) did they succeed in making a grant based on that rate of quit rent.   All their other grants, like Ludwell's and those which had preceded his, are based on 'the rent the King accepted;' that is to say, two shillings per hundred acres.   And so the practice continued in the proprietary office down to 1781.

2.   *They have changed 'patents into conveyances, and entry of Right is totally left off so that one of the great motives, to wit the Peopling of the Country, which first induced the King to make this grant, is quite laid aside.'*

This was a rhetorical statement that the head right was not recognised in the proprietary.   There was never any 'entry of right' either above or below the Rappahannock.   In Virginia proper the planter could not make an entry even of his head right until specifically authorized by resolution of the Council exercising a sound discretion.   In the proprietary the agents exercised a similar discretion.

Practically, in the great majority of cases, this could not have been a real objection.   While the proprietary agents could, and doubtless did, show favoritism in reserving choice lands for their friends and families, so did the Council within its jurisdiction.   On the other hand, the urgent demands of their principals for increased quit rents and the resulting increase of their own commissions stimulated the agents to seat as many planters as they could.   It is not likely that any deserving man, able to comply with the rules of the office, was ever denied the right of entry within the proprietary. Indeed, the Virginia government complained later that the Northern Neck agents seated many men who could not have secured a patent below the Rappahannock.

3. *They 'sell the lands now taken up at the full value and some times a great deal more.'*

This is the complement of the last previous complaint, being directed at the undoubted fact that there was no limitation in law upon the proprietor's demand of 'composition' as the condition of an entry. Practically, however, there was a limitation by reason of the competition with the head right territory to secure immigration.

The maximum terms of 'composition' which obtained in the proprietary from its origin to its extinction were stated by Philip Ludwell in his grants, as follows:

'five Shillings as a fine for every hundred acres for all quantities of land that shall be taken up above one hundred acres to Six hundred acres; and for all quantities of land above six hundred acres after the rate of ten shillings for every hundred acres.'

At the end of the seventeenth century none but the bottom lands were seated in Virginia. Considering the yield of tobacco by such bottoms on the creeks of the Potomac and Rappahannock well into the eighteenth century it would seem that the suggestion can hardly have been candid that in 1695 they were not worth a penny an acre, especially when that penny was paid, when paid at all, like the quit rents, in tobacco at the exchange value of 'trash.'

4. *In the matter of escheats they refuse to be bound by the Virginia practice of allowing the possessor to redeem for a composition of 2 lbs. tobo. per acre; and they grant escheats in futuro.*

This was personal criticism of Messrs. Brent and Fitzhugh. Their grant book shows that with the aid of the judicial
procedure known as 'office found' they squeezed their neighbours in the matter of excheats to the full limit of their opportunity. The irony of the complaint, like that which followed
against large grants, is, however, that it was formulated in the
Assembly by Robert Carter. When he succeeded to the proprietary agency, precisely similar charges were brought against
him.

Virginia had Francis Moryson to thank for her provision
of law in the matter of redemption of escheated lands. It was
he who with characteristic enlightenment formulated the tentative rules of 1662, and it was again he who crystallized the
ultimate standard in the charter of 1676 (*Cf.* Hening, ii. 136
and 532). There the provision reads as follows:

'all lands possest by any subject inhabiting in Virginia
which is escheated, or shall escheat unto us, our heirs and successors, shall and may be injoyed by such inhabitant or possessor, his heirs and assigns for ever, paying two pounds of tobacco composition for every acre; which is the rate set by our
governour according to our instructions to him in that behalf.'

For all that Brent and Fitzhugh were fit targets for attack
on this record, it does not follow that they were unprecedented
monsters of moral obliquity. The address was formulated for
the eye of a remote tribunal which was not expected to go beyond the record. On the other hand, the Hartwell, Chilton and
Blair tract, written two years after this address to the Crown,
testified that whatever was the rule, the actual Virginia practice
in the matter of escheats was subject, as much as that of
the agents, to the criticism of favoritism.

'When a man dies seized of land in fee wihout will or heirs,'
said that able state paper in 1697, 'such land escheats to the
King, and is thus disposed of: By the King's charter the
person in possession has the right of the grant but of late
it depends on the Governor's favour, who accepts that one
of the petitions for the benefit of the escheat which best pleases
him, and underwrites it thus 'This petition is granted, paying

Composition to the Auditor according to law.' The Governor's warrant then issues to the escheator of the precinct, who makes inquisition and finds the office by a jury of twelve men. This inquisition being returned to the Secretary's office lies there nine months, so that anyone concerned may traverse the office, and if no one appears, a patent is passed according to the petitioner's request. The Escheator's fee is £5 sterling, and the composition by the Charter is 2 lbs. of tobacco per acre.'

Although Robert Carter did not himself observe it during his agency and was entirely within his rights in declining to do so, the Virginia practice of composition for escheats ultimately obtained in the proprietary. That it had the support of public opinion appears from the fact that it was restated in the land act of 1705 and it may be assumed that the same power induced Lord Fairfax to apply it after 1736. Being resident in the colony, the last proprietor was more open to such influences than any of his predecessors in the management of the estate, and it is another evidence of his anxiety always to be considered fair in dealing with his neighbours that he accepted the standard composition for escheats.

5. *They reserve the right of re-entry in case of 2 years' default of rent.*

This purely practical reservation made its appearance in principle in the Brent Town grant of 1687. Originally based on nine months' default in payment of rent, Philip Ludwell enlarged the grace to two years and so it continued through the remaining years of the proprietary. In 1695 this was otherwise unprecedented in Virginia, where the patents had never contained such a reservation. The objection to it is not convincing of hardship except on the principle that tax dodging had become a franchise below the Rappahannock. That that was soon to be the deliberate opinion of the Virginia government appears, as will be shown, in its adoption a few years later of the proprietary practice here objected to.

6. *'And for lands lapsing for wante of Seating none such will happen, for in the Conveyances of the sd. L'ds Agents there*

*is not any Limitation upon that accounte, and accordingly a
man may hold 50,000 or more Acres of land by a secure title,
and that without so much as actually seating or building upon
any part of it.'*

This pointed out an enduring difference between Virginia
and Northern Neck practice; but it is difficult to see how a
popular grievance could be made of it.

From the earliest times, the Virginia patents had contained a provision for reversion in case of failure to seat or
plant. The earliest surviving Northern Neck grant followed
that precedent in 1675; but it disappeared from the Northern
Neck practice with the Brent Town grant of 1687, never to
reappear. From the point of view of the public interest, this
was undoubtedly a defect in the Northern Neck practice, but
from the point of view of the individual grantee it was an advantage in the Northern Neck grant over the Virginia patent.

The reference to the unproductive holding of '50,000 or
more acres of land' was another fling at the agents as distinguished from their principals. Prior to 1695 George Brent
had laid out Brent Town and William Fitzhugh had laid out
'Ravensworth,' but neither of these great tracts had been
seated. The objection Virginia could justly make to these
reservations for future exploitation was that they set an
example which most well to do Virginians followed as soon as
they had opportunity. But it should be remembered that both
Governors Gooch and Dinwiddie defended large land grants
in principle as enabling the immigrant to secure from the
grantee a small plantation without incurring the heavy, and in
some cases prohibitive, cost of office fees.

[7. *Mineral rights.*]

The only important difference between a Virginia patent
and the Northern Neck grant to which the Address of 1695
does not refer is in the reservation of mineral rights. In 1695
this had not become a practical question. If, despite the pro-

visions made in the act of 1713 for mining, as an alternative to 'planting,' in 'saving' a patent, and the actual iron mining operations later undertaken by Spotswood, Hunter and others in several parts of the colony, Stith could say in 1747 that 'Virginia is not a country of mines,' much more was that true at the end of the seventeenth century. The original hope had been, however, to make of Virginia what Spain had made of her earlier adventures in Central and South America; and James I's first charter for Virginia put emphasis on the intended 'search for all manner of Mines of Gold, Silver and Copper.' The Crown then reserved, in addition to a 'royalty' of one-fifth of gold and silver, one fifteenth of all copper mined; but by the charters of 1609 and 1612 this was limited to the customary one-fifth of the 'royal mines' only. In this right the Virginia Company transferred to the planter his 'due share of all mines and minerals;' and the precedent being followed, the holder of land under a Virginia patent became uniformly entitled to all minerals he might mine on his own land, subject only to the 'royalties' of gold and silver.

In like manner the Northern Neck charters carried grants of minerals, (more elaborately specified as gold, silver, lead, tin, iron, copper, stone and coal), subject only to the 'royalty' on gold and silver. When the proprietors came to deal with this question in their grants they were not so liberal as the Company. They reserved not only the 'royalty' for the benefit of the Crown, but, as a feudality for their own benefit, all the remainder of the gold and silver and in addition a share of other minerals. The rate of such reservation varied during the seventeenth century and only became crystalized in Robert Carter's grant form in 1704, viz:

1675	1687	1690	1694	1704-1781
All gold and silver.	All gold, silver, copper, tin and lead.	'Royalties' plus 1/4 gold and 1/5 silver; 1/3 tin, copper, iron, lead and coal.	All gold and silver; 1/3 lead, tin and iron (omitting coal).	All gold and silver; 1/3 lead, copper, tin, coal and iron.

Until well into the eighteenth century no mines of any kind were opened in the proprietary and these provisions stood as mere badges of a feudal law which knew nothing of industrial problems. When copper was discovered in the territory now known as Fairfax, they became practical bars to exploitation by anyone who could not secure a waiver of the proprietary reservations. Thus it was that the Frying Pan Company, organized in 1730 by Robert Carter and Mann Page, alone was able to undertake actual copper mining. A generation later a number of iron mines were opened in the proprietary. Compared with the Spotswood mines below the Rappahannock, their history is one of economic struggle, and clearly demonstrates that the proprietary reservations were too great to leave a margin of profit to the miner.

It was during the consulship of Spotswood that a substantial accord was accomplished between those dissonant practices of the rival land offices which Robert Carter's legislative address of 1695 served to define. This came about as a consequence of the suppression, under the vigorous criticism of Messrs. Hartwell, Chilton and Blair and of Spotswood himself, of the speculation in head rights which had grown until it became a scandal.

We have seen that in 1699, when the indian territories known as Pamunkey Neck and Blackwater Swamp were about to be opened for seating, the Crown withheld authority until assured that there would be no jobbing in head rights. As it happened, the tide of immigration was then running so low that few head rights were on the market, and to this was added the fact of 'the Treasury of the Country for the support of the government being very low' also. The reversion to the obsolete 'treasury right,' in which the Council found the solution of both these problems, involved far reaching changes in the practice of the colonial land office. There was introduced a provision for a 'fine' at the rate of ten shillings per hundred acres as the consideration for a grant in lieu of the head right, and the new patent form contained a clause for stimulating the payment of quit rents by reserving the right of re-entry after three years of default. The consequence of these changes was the conversion of the sacred head right into a museum specimen. Henceforth practically all Virginia patents were based on the new treasury right.

When these questions were under discussion in the Council, an influential member of that body had recently taken over the proprietary agency and was rapidly putting the estate on an income-producing footing. Purged of his jealousy of William Fitzhugh, Robert Carter had had opportunity to learn the convenience as well as the efficacy of the conveyancing forms and practices which a few years before had kindled his wrath in the Assembly. That it was his advice which prevailed in the Council is apparent on comparison of the proprietary practice with what was now done in the Secretary's office. Virginia had taken over, not only in principle but in detail, two of the things she had previously denounced as 'strange and exorbitant.' The differences in the terms under which the individual henceforth held land by patent and grant were now no more than that the government form contained the provision for lapse in case of failure to seat, which was never in the Northern Neck form, but in compensation the Virginia form vested a larger mineral right than could be acquired in the Northern Neck.

It is at once significant and curious that this accord in the practices of the rival land offices did not result from alteration of the proprietary practices, but, on the contrary, in the substantial adoption of those practices by the Virginia Government and the spread of them throughout the province; and that, too, on the motion of the author of the Address of 1695. It would be claiming for Robert Carter too great prevision to say that his part in the reforms expressed in the land law of 1705 was planned to accomplish the economic consequences of that legislation; but the fact remains that it seems to have established the Northern Neck proprietary beyond further peradventure.

To push home the point, it will suffice to compare the circumstances of the immigration up the Potomac during the seventeenth century, and that up the Shenandoah in the eighteenth. Both set in with the economic impetus that lands might be acquired at less cost in Virginia than in Maryland or Pennsylvania. In the earlier case the stream was dissipated at its source; in the later case it flowed in a torrent. There were, of course, many reasons for this difference, but there can be no doubt that an important one was the modification of public opinion of the Northern Neck grant. In the seventeenth century that was held to be anathema as compared with the Virginia patent; in 1750 Lord Fairfax's land office was crowded with applicants for his grants, which all now agreed were as favorable as those contemporaneously issued from the Virginia government's office at Williamsburg.

As the terms of the Northern Neck grants which accomplished success in the Valley were identical with those which were held to be responsible for the delay in seating Stafford, the indignation expressed in that earlier time against the practices of the proprietary office seems, as we look back on it, to be, like many other legislative histrionics, before and since, no more than the bait of the fisher in troubled waters.

Alexander Brown's thesis that, by its *Orders and Constitutions* of 1618, the Virginia Company established 'the first republic in America' finds significant support in the provisions of that state paper for a 'commonwealth' of land. That the political principles therein implicit survived, in the colony, the dissolution of the Company may be attributed in no small measure to Charles I's acceptance, after long hesitation, of the Company's key institution of the head right. The moment of that decision (1634) was thus a critical one in the political history of the colony; for the recognition of the head right was not contemporaneously counteracted by provision to cover the quit rents into the exchequer, and that failure resulted in negligent collection of those badges of suzerainty and the ultimate acknowledgment by the King that the quit rents belonged to the colony.

As this was going further even than Sir Edwin Sandys had imagined, it is worth while to rehearse the terms of so vital an acknowledgment. On August 11, 1681,[213] a committee of the Privy Council, having considered the Arlington charter of 1673, recommended that henceforth H. M. reserve all colonial quit rents 'intirely for the support of the respective governments therein;' whereupon Charles II

'declared in Council that he would henceforth make no grant of any Quit Rents to any person . . . that they might be reserved for the Support of the Government in the places aforesaid *as they were originally intended.*'

Caveats against passing future grants of quit rents were accordingly ordered lodged in all Crown offices, and, following the surrender of the Arlington charter of 1673, which was accomplished soon thereafter (1684), the Virginia quit rents were appropriated for the support of the Virginia government.

This was in effect a royal expression of the principle that Virginia land was 'commonwealth,' that the planters themselves were entitled to the fruits of their own pains and industry in conquering the forest. It is not difficult to imagine the ferment which such a grace introduced into the political intelligence of the average burgess as he took his seat in the Virginia Assembly. He was thereby furnished with a master precedent for a working theory that the Crown might be successfully resisted in matters affecting colonial pocket books. Against such a consciousness, the subsequent argument of Hartwell, Chilton and Blair that the 'waste' lands of Virginia belonged to the Crown and Spotswood's alteration of the form of the land patent to give colour to that theory were gestures and practically without effect. The 'waste' lands of Virginia remained 'commonwealth' to the end of the chapter, even in the Northern Neck. Richard Bland and Richard Henry Lee, not to speak of Patrick Henry and Thomas Jefferson, were thus the inheritors of a self-conscious political sentiment which had its origin in the seventeenth century.

NOTES AND SOURCES

1. Spotswood's dispatches make this point clear. On February 11, 1712/13 (*Spotswood Letters*, ii, 14) he wrote:
'And it seems strange to me, when I read over the records of the Country, to find such unaccountable proceedings in the granting of land, as have been practised heretofore: [that] the General Courts, where the Governor has no negative voice and must be concluded in his judgment by the majority of the bench, should be allowed to pass grants of land, and even in manner so dishonourable as to order the Governor to grant a patent; which nevertheless was the practice before my time. Every one who had a mind to a tract of land, vested in the Crown either originally or by lapse or escheat, claimed a right to have a patent for it upon his petition; without acknowledging any right in the Governor to dispense the favours of the Crown according to the merits and qualifications of the person. This custom being suffered so long to prevail is now pleaded as the Right of the people, and all restrictions of that method looked upon as so many infringements of their liberty; and her Majesty's favour seems to them a new term with which they are not acquainted, or at least they forget the meaning of.'
On February 7, 1715/16 (*ibid.*, ii, 216), reporting that he had forbidden entries 'for all tracts exceeding 400 acres' without leave 'first obtained from the Governor in Council to enter for the same,' he made the sarcastic, but none the less significant, comment, 'this, I confess, is a restraint on the ancient liberty which some people here made use of.'

2. *Cf.* Gould, *The Land System in Maryland* (Johns Hopkins University Studies, 1913, p. 9): 'Following the plan which had worked so successfully in Virginia, Lord Baltimore provided in his early conditions of plantation for the granting of land to those who would transport settlers into the colony. By each grant there was reserved to the proprietor a perpetual quit-rent, which, though originally payable in wheat, was fixed in 1671 at four shillings sterling per hundred acres. In 1683 transportation of settlers ceased to be the basis for the granting of lands, which were thereafter obtainable only on the payment of a purchase price, called caution money, of two hundred pounds of tobacco per hundred acres. This was raised in 1684 to two hundred and forty pounds, which rate was doubled during the royal period. In 1717 the purchase price was changed to money at the rate of one penny for each pound of tobacco, making forty shillings sterling per hundred acres.
'These terms remained unchanged during the continuance of the commutation law, but after its expiration in 1733 an increase in the land rates again became very tempting to the proprietor. By the instructions to Edmund Jennings, judge of the land office in that year, the purchase price was left at forty shillings sterling per hundred acres, but the quit-rent was raised from four shillings to ten shillings. Under these terms the number of land grants showed a sharp decrease, so that in 1738 the four shilling quit-rent was restored,

but the purchase price was advanced from £2 to £5 sterling per hundred acres. At the same time the land officials were informed that these were but minimum rates, and that higher rates should be demanded wherever, in the judgment of the governor, the secretary, and the judge of the land office, the desirability of the land would admit of it. In practice, however, increased rates were seldom, if ever, demanded. After 1738 there was no further change in the land rates until the Revolution.'

It was the relatively higher cost of acquiring land in Pennsylvania and Maryland as compared with Virginia which started out of Pennsylvania into the Shenandoah Valley that fateful flood of immigration of the Scotch-Irish and Germans who were eventually to rend Virginia and alter her civilization; and it was the unprecedented Virginia land tax during the decade following 1755 (Hening, vi, 463, ff.; repealed, 1768, *ibid.*, viii, 298) which drove on an overflow of that tide into the Carolina piedmont and so established the social character of that region also.

3. Hening, x, 35. There is a characteristically lucid discussion of this act in relation to other colonial and revolutionary land laws by Benjamin Watkins Leigh in his *Revised Code of the Laws of Virginia,* 1819, ii, 332 ff. It was passed when Virginia was in greater need of soldiers and funds to carry on the war of independence than she was of immigrants. The head right was accordingly abolished after it had been in existence for 161 years, but the treasury right was renewed at a new (and higher) rate.

It is of interest that the new federal government went through the same process with respect to the public domain, but ultimately reverted to the head right. 'The primary conception of Congress,' says Mr. S. V. Proudfit (*Public Land System of the U. S.,* 1923) 'in dealing with the public lands was the realization of the largest possible cash return for their sale to meet the immediate necessity of national enterprise . . . Since that time . . . a broad conception of the proper foundation of our national institutions . . . gradually came to be recognized and took form in later statutes that substantially abandoned the cash sale proposition and adopted a theory based on the enhancement of agricultural values in which the entire nation would ultimately profit . . . The homestead act of May 20, 1862 (12 Stat., 392) was the logical successor of the pre-emption law in which the home was made the unit of development and citizenship, a prerequisite to the right of final entry.' It would be curious to trace the influence of the Virginia tradition in this process.

4. Brown, *Genesis,* 52, at p. 62. The Virginia charters of 1606, 1609 and 1612 were first printed in full by Stith in 1747, but may be studied to best advantage in Mr. Alexander Brown's great book.

The 'manor of East Greenwich' was the royal palace of Greenwich which was James I's residence.

The American, accustomed to his private title 'in fee simple,' is apt to forget the theory of the common law, that in respect to lands, such an estate is the peculiar attribute of the Sovereign. In his stately way, Blackstone wrote at the time of the American Revolution, 'A subject hath only the usufruct and not the absolute property of the Soil . . . it being a received, and now undeniable, principle in the law that all the lands in England are holden mediately or immediately of the King.' Of the tenure by free socage he adds that it 'consisted of free and honourable services; but such as were liquidated and reduced to an absolute certainty.' (The best modern discussion of socage is that in Pollock and Maitland, *History of English Law,* 2d ed., i, 291, ff.) In the Virginia practice throughout the colonial period this service was limited to the reservation of a specific quit rent. By the revolutionary act of 1777 (Hening, ix, 359) it was provided 'and that lands may not be . . . subject to any feudal tenure . . . all lands within this Commonwealth shall henceforth be exempted and discharged from the payment of all royal quit rents.' This act of the new sovereign operated as the release in the form of conveyance, then usual, known as the 'lease and release :' it vested in the holder of Virginia lands, what no Englishman had, the fee simple : but incidentally it opened the Pandora's box of land taxes.

5. Brown, *Genesis,* 208, at p. 230.

6. *Force's Tracts,* i, Nos. 6 and 7. Mr. Alexander Brown was of opinion that the author of this able paper of 1609, as well as its supplement, *The New Life of Virginea* (1612), was Robert Johnson, of the Grocers Company, later Sheriff and Alderman of London, who was the close associate of Sir Thomas Smythe in the leadership of the 'merchants party' in the Virginia Company. If these conjectures be justified, he may also have been the author of the *Brief Declaration* (1616) which is printed in Brown, *Genesis,* ii, 775.

7. *Journals H. B.,* 1619-1659, p. 6; and *cf.* Brown, *First Republic,* p. 293. The *Orders and Constitutions* were published in June, 1620, by the Council for Virginia (*Force's Tracts,* iii, No. 6), but the somewhat different form in which they reached Virginia and were considered by the Assembly is in Sir George Yeardley's instructions of 1618, which have survived in the *Randolph MS.* (*Va. Mag.,* ii, 154). With this important document should be read the *Declaration against the Company,* formulated in 1642 (Hening, i, 230), when it was proposed to reinstate the Company. Virginia had found that once the Crown admitted the head right the colony was freer than ever it could be under a Company.

8. The precedent of the joining of the 'Council of State' with the Governor in the power to grant lands, thus inaugurated by the Orders and Constitutions of 1618, was uniformly followed by the royal instructions after the Crown assumed the government of the colony. This went a long way to establish the principle that Virginia lands were 'commonwealth' in the disposition of the planters themselves rather than of the Crown; for it made it possible for the Council to out vote the Governor in authorizing land grants. That principle was settled in 1666 (Hening, ii, 253. See the discussion of the incident *ante,* p. 31). For this consideration Berkeley was unable to comply with Charles II's instructions to desist from issuing patents for lands in the Northern Neck after the Restoration even had he been inclined to do so, which may be doubted; and Spotswood, feeling the same restraint in 1713, denounced the practice as 'dishonourable' to the Governor (See *ante.,* note 1).

9. *Patents,* 1 : 1. With this should be compared George Sandys' patent of 1624 (*Patents,* 1 : 12, and printed in Brown, *First Republic,* p. 605) which will be found to vary in minor detail, indicating that the form had not yet become definitely crystalized.

Thomas Hothersall was a 'citizen and grocer' of London and came to Virginia in April, 1621, in the *Margaret & John*. He thus had the honour not only of taking part in a notable fight with two Spanish men of war at Nevis, but of recording that adventure for posterity. In his patent he is described as of 'Paspehay,' because he first established himself in the region of the indians of that name, above Jamestown, which was later included in James City County; but the census of 1625 shows him then living on his patent at Blunt Point (Warwick). See *Va. Mag.*, i, 83; Brown, *First Republic*, 416, 622; *Purchas his Pilgrimes* (Glasgow, 1906), xix, 135; Smith's Works (ed. Arber), ii, 544.

10. *Patents*, 1 : 47, to Thomas Bouldin.

11. Rymer, *Foedera*, xvii, 618; Hazard, *Hist. Collections*, i, 189.

12. *Va. Mag.*, vii, 132.

13. *Cal. State Papers*, Am. & W. I., 1574-1660, p. 79.

14. Rymer, xviii, 311; Hazard, i, 230. In Rymer's print this commission is dated March 4, 1 Car. I, but his print of Harvey's commission of March 26, 3 Car., I, recites it as dated 'March fowerteenth' as it is in the Virginia land patents which were founded on it (*Cf.* Bruce, *Econ. Hist.*, i, 515). March 14, 1625/6 is also the date which Mr. Conway Robinson gave to this commission in his transcript of it from the lost Council Journal (*Va. Mag.*, xiii, 298).

15. *Va. Mag.*, ii, 393. The letter of the company 'after the massacre' here referred to is that of August 1, 1622, making merely temporary provision for those whom the indians had driven off their own plantations. It is printed in Neill, *Virginia Company*, p. 322.

16. *Patents*, 1 : 49.

17. As in the case of Yeardley's commission, there is a curious confusion in the books with reference to the date of Harvey's first commission. Sainsbury (*Cal. Am. & W. I.*, 1574-1660, p. 88) gives it March 22, 1628; Rymer (xviii, 98), followed by Hazard, (i, 234), printing the full text give the attestation 'Witness ourself at Westminster the six and twentieth Day of Marche,' without year, either *Domini* or *Regis*. In Harvey's commission of 1636, infra, as well as in the Virginia land records, the commission here in question is recited as dated March 26 'in the third year of our Raign.' This, read with its own recital of Yeardley's death, fixes the year as 1628. But note that in some of the Virginia patents (e. g., *Patents*, 1 : 114) this commission is perversely recited as 'bearing date the six and twentieth day of March in the third yeare of his Majties Raigne that now is, one Thousand six hundred *twentie seven*.' This, however, seems to be no more than a clerical error.

18. *Va. Mag.*, vii, 267.

19. *Va. Mag.*, vii, 369.

20. e. g., *Patents*, 1 : 104, to Capt. Robert Felgate as 'due to him by the transportacon of himself, his sonn and fower servants, who came in the *William and John* one thousand six hundred twenty and eight.'

21. e. g., *Patents*, 1 : 114.

22. *Journals H. B.*, 1619-60, p. 55. This suggestion, it will be noted, was a renewal of the principle of the Company that the more 'ancient' was the planter the greater should be his dividend.

23. *Cal. State Papers*, Am. & W. I., 1574-1660, p. 175.

24. *Acts P. C.*, Colonial, i, 203; *Cal. Am. & W. I.*, 1574-1660, p. 185.

25. *Patents*, 1 : 158.

26. Rymer, xx, 3; *Va. Mag.*, ix, 37.

27. The text of these instructions has not survived. The date is recited not only in the Virginia patent books as here quoted, but in Harvey's dispatch of January 18, 1638/9 (*Cal. Am. & W. I.*, 1574-1680, p. 287).

28. e. g., *Patents*, 1 : 410.

29. *Va. Mag.*, xi, 54.

30. *Va. Mag.*, ii, 281, at p. 285.

31. *Patents*, 2 : 157. This is Bartholomew Hoskins' grant of January 1, 1645/6. The record being abbreviated, the text is derived from the original patent *penes me*. It is similar to *Patents*, 1 : 702, issued by Wyatt in 1639, which is printed by Dr. Bruce (*Economic History*, i, 515).

The endorsements on this Hoskins patent illustrate a simple conveyancing practice which grew up in Virginia in the seventeenth century. In order to save fees the planters conveyed their lands by simple endorsement on the original patent. At intervals the landowner would surrender this patent at the Secretary's office and take out a new one in his own name.

32. This act, being missing, is not in Hening.

33. Hening, i, 364.

34. *Patents*, 3 : 137. This is the form of one of Governor Richard Bennet's patents of 1652. The record is condensed, but the original survives in the vagrom collection of muniments in the State Library at Richmond. Dr. Palmer printed it (*Cal. Va. State Papers,* i, p. 1) and characteristically mangled it.

35. This act also is missing.

36. Hening, ii, 245. It appears from this report (with which should be read Hening, iii, 524; v, 417) that in addition to the land grants sealed by the Company prior to 1624 many other early land patents are now missing because they were not recorded.

37. *Va. Mag.*, iii, 15. The exemption of quit rents for seven years, originally allowed by the Virginia Company, was formally re-asserted by the Assembly in 1640 (Hening, i, 228, 280) and accepted by the Crown in the approval of that act. But already the amount of the quit rents had become of importance and the early loose practice in the collecting of them had been tightened up (See Howard Horsey's petition of 1639 to be appointed Receiver General [i. e. Treasurer] in succession to Jerome Hawley, *Cal. Am. & W. I.*, 1674-1660, p. 302).

38. *Patents*, 5 : 293. This is George Barker's regrant of October 27, 1663. The record being abbreviated, the text is derived from the

original patent among the Ludwell MSS. in the possession of the Virginia Historical Society.

39. *Journals H. B.*, 1660-93, p. 37; Hening, ii, 253.

40. Burk, *History of Virginia*, ii, Appendix, p. xlviii.

41. *Pat. Roll*, 28 Car., II, pt. 1, No. 11; Hening, ii, 532. The record of the earlier abortive charter is in *Acts P. C.*, Colonial, i, 629, 636, 661. Although the charter of 1676 was much less than Virginia expected, its confirmation of the head right proved to be the bar to the attempt in Queen Anne's time to weaken that right. For this consideration it is interesting that it was Culpeper who procured the sealing of the charter of 1676 (See Thomas Ludwell's testimony in Burk, ii, 247). Thus it was that two of the best hated of Virginia's royal Governors, Harvey and Culpeper, were both instruments in preserving one of Virginia's most important franchises.

42. Hening, ii, 418.

43. The indian treaty of May 29, 1677, referred to in *Cal. Am. & W. I.*, 1677-80, No. 272, p. 97, is printed in *Va. Mag.*, xiv, 289.
That the intention of land speculation entered into the indian treaty of 1677 from its inception appears in Francis Moryson's pleasant letter to Secretary Ludwell of November 28, 1677 (Burk, ii, 268). 'When the articles of peace were ordered to be printed,' he wrote from London, 'some complained there was too much land taken up, which gave a great minister a hint to say that there was a sore place under that, which was to raise great fees to the Secretary.'

44. *Journals H. B.*, 1660-93, pp. 115, 474, 477; 1695-1702, pp. 23, 281 ff.

45. The provision for lands in the charter of William & Mary College of February 8, 1692/3, is interesting in relation to the thesis of the Virginia commonwealth in land. It was given the form of a gift by King William and Queen Mary, but, in fact, it was no more than a renewal of what the Company had planned by the *Orders and Constitutions* of 1618.

46. The Hartwell, Chilton and Blair *Present State of Virginia* was compiled in October, 1697, as a report for the Lords of Trade, and the original remains in the C. O. records. Printed as a pamphlet in aid of William and Mary College in 1727 (London, John Wyat: See the copy in the Virginia State Library) and reproduced in Massachusetts Historical Society *Collections*, Series 1, vol. v, p. 124; this most illuminating, if most tory, of all Virginia tracts may be studied conveniently in *Cal. Am. & W. I.*, 1696-97, No. 1396, p. 641.

47. The traffic in head rights here described began before 1642, when the Assembly (Hening, i, 274, 444; ii, 95) ordered that all such rights should be recorded in the County Courts before dividends could be based on them. This served, as Hartwell shows, not so much to check the traffic as to concentrate the market in the Secretary's office.
Spotswood confirms and supplements (*Spotswood Letters*, ii, 15, 22) Hartwell's enumeration of the steps in the process of multiplication of these 'rights.' He says that he had come upon one case of '500 acres granted for one importation,' and he adds another specification of the abuse:

'And because Persons imported into the Northern Neck are allowed by the Proprietors no land for their importation, and therefore it hath been a custom to prove their rights and assign them over for taking up land in that part of the colony held of her Majesty, I have put a stop to that Traffique by disallowing all rights for persons imported into that part of the Government; it being unreasonable in my opinion that persons who imploy themselves solely in improving the land of the Proprietors should be entitled to receive a benefit of her Majesty's land.'

48. Under the act of 1662 (Hening, ii, 99) the quit rent of 2s. per hundred acres was paid in tobacco at the fixed commuted rate of 2d. per pound. Hartwell's statement that the quit rent tobacco brought in the market only 5s. per hundred (or little more than a ha' penny a pound) is evidence that only the worst tobacco was tendered in payment of quit rents.

49. '*Seating and Planting*:' Hartwell's sneer at the definition of seating and planting authorized by the act of 1666 (Hening, ii, 244), which was still in force when he wrote, was echoed by Spotswood in the denunciation of it as 'a sham condition' (*Spotswood Letters*, ii, 15). Goaded by the allusion to the 'hog house,' the Revisors of 1705 proposed (Hening, iii, 313) a definition of the house to be erected as 'one house of wood after the usuall manner of building in this colony, being at least in length twelve foot and in breadth twelve foot;' but the veto of the Land Act of 1705 left the abuse unchecked, even by this mild reform. It thus remained for Spotswood, under the provisions of Lord Orkney's instructions, to push through an act which laid down the principles of 'seating and planting' which obtained during the remainder of the colonial period. His act of 1713 (Hening, iv, 39) directed the surveyor of lands to be patented to certify what proportion of such lands was plantable, what fit for pasture, and what 'stony or rocky' and for that reason not to be classified in either of the other two categories. Different standards of seating and planting were set up as the condition of 'saving' each of these kinds of land, viz:

1. If the land was partly plantable and partly pasturage, then for every fifty acres patented, the obligation of the patentee was: as to the plantable portion either (a) 'to clear, tend and work three acres at the least,' or (b) 'to clear and drain three acres of swamp or sunken grounds or drain three acres of marsh;' and, as to the pasturage, to stock and for three years to maintain 'three neat cattle or six sheep or goats.'

2. If the land was pasturage but in no part plantable 'without manuring and improving the same,' then, in addition to the prescribed stock of cattle for each fifty acres the patentee was required 'to erect and build on some part of the said tract one good dwelling house after the manner of Virginia building to contain at least twenty foot in length and sixteen foot in breadth.'

3. If, however, the land was 'stony or rocky grounds not fit for planting or pasturage,' then the employment thereon of 'one good able hand' for three years 'digging any stone quarry, coal or other mines' was declared to save 100 acres.

In 1720 (Hening, iv, 81) the act of 1713 was amended by declaring that there were other kinds of 'cultivation and improvements' which were 'equally beneficially,' wherefore it was stipulated that fifty acres might be 'saved' by every expenditure in such improvement of £10. By the revisal of 1748 (Hening, v, 424) this minimum investment was reduced to £5.

50. Nicholson's instructions are *Cal. Am. & W. I.,* 1697-98, No. 819, at p. 423. See *ibid.,* 1701, pp. 542, 546, 553 for his vain efforts to carry them out, including his refusal to approve a bill to quiet certain particular titles in Pamunkey Neck, on the ground that they represented purchases from the Queen of Pamunkey and so were contrary to his instructions. Nott's instructions (1705) are *Cal. Am. & W. I.,* 1704-05, No. 1051, at p. 494. It was in protest of them that the Council formulated that important 'Account of the method of taking up and patenting Land in Virginia' (*Cal. Am. & W. I.,* 1706-08, p. 205, 207; *W. & M. Quar.,* 2d Series, iii, 137), which effectually reasserted the charter status of the headright. Although this paper did not reach England until after the instructions of 1705 had been renewed to Hunter in 1707 (*Cal. Am. & W. I.,* 1706-08, No. 871, p. 422), when it was considered they were promptly withdrawn. See the additional instructions to Hunter of 1709 (C. O., 5: 1344, carried forward in a slightly different form as article 82 of the instructions of 1715 to Lord Orkney, *Va. Mag.,* xxi, 233). The incident was rehearsed in detail by the Lords of Trade in *Acts P. C.,* Colonial, ii, p. 585.

51. The land act of 1705 is in Hening, iii, 304. The objection to it by the Lords of Trade and the proceedings in the Privy Council on April 17, 1707 for disallowance, are in *Cal. Am. & W. I.,* 1706-08, pp. 406, 421.

Following the note in Hening, iii, 304, Mr. B. W. Leigh (*Code* 1819, ii, 337) points out the error of the Revisals of 1733 and 1752 in attributing the repeal of the act of 1705 to Virginia legislation, but himself goes beyond the record in asserting that all such parts of the act of 1705 as were not within the purview of the acts of 1710 and 1748 (Hening, iii, 517; v, 408) continued in effect. If this had been a correct judgment, then the form of patent used in and after 1710 should have followed that prescribed by the act of 1705, which it did not, as a comparison will show.

52. *Patents,* 10: 1.

53. For Spotswood's individual patents see *Patents* 10: 290, with which *cf. Spotswood Letters,* ii, 215; *Patents,* 11: 145; 12: 433; 14: 378, 381; the petition from Spotsylvania in 1724 in *Cal. Va. State Papers,* i, 208; and the proceedings of the Privy Council by which these claims were ultimately confirmed in *Acts P. C.,* Colonial, iii, 168; vi, 188.

54. *Spotswood Letters,* ii, 15 and *cf. ibid.,* 216, where he puts his emphasis on 'the great abuse of some persons entering for vast tracts containing much more land than they would be able to cultivate and holding them by the connivance or confederacy of the Surveyors for many years without offering either to sue out patents or sometimes even so much as to survey the same: so that for want of Patents I found the Crown must loose its Quit Rents and for want of bounds the people must a long time be debarred from the adjacent lands.'

55. For a discussion of the Virginia use of the term 'manor' see *Landmarks of Old Prince William.*

56. C. O., 5 : 1321, p. 213.

57. *Dinwiddie Papers,* i, 371.

58. One searches the patent books in vain for a true head right patent after 1715. Some of the grants made by the Council in the Shenandoah Valley in 1730 to immigrants from the north were, indeed, based on seating so many 'families' but on analysis this will be found to be rather a 'military right' than a 'head right', for the purpose was to secure protection for the frontier, not to recognize a franchise vested in a citizen of Virginia.

59. *Patents,* 1 : 114. *Cf. Va. Mag.,* ii, 186. The 'bill of adventure' was fortunately recorded with the patent.

60. Brown, *First Republic,* p. 289.

61. Mr. Alexander Brown collected from the vestiges of the early records of the Virginia Company the testimonies for the earliest land grants in Virginia, all of which were based on the treasury right. Beginning with Simon Codrington's patent of 1616, he included the list of the 'particular plantations' created down to 1624. See *First Republic,* pp. 233, 235, 256, 291, 628. There is another such list in *Va. Mag.,* vi, 372.

62. The litigation of *Cary and Brewer v. Harlowe* in 1659 (Hening, i, 506, 529, 548; *Journals H. B.,* 1619-1659, p. 113; *The Devon Carys,* p. 610) concerning the 'common,' granted by the Company to Stanley Hundred in what became Warwick County, shows that after the dissolution those areas passed into private ownership with the other Hundred lands.

63. *Patents,* 1 : 410. The Smyth of Nibley MSS. (*Bulletin N. Y. Public Library,* i, 186; iii, 167, 208) are rich in material for the history of Berkeley Hundred from its organization in September, 1620, with two resident 'Governors General' to the destruction of plantations and the hopes of the founders by the massacre of 1622. For the purchasers of 1636 Capt. William Tucker (1589-1640) of Kiccotan, and his brothers-in-law, Maurice and George Thompson, see Brown, *Genesis,* ii, 1034; D. N. B. (re-issue), xix, 1212, and the note on the Tucker family in *Va. Mag.,* xvii, 394. The loss of the Charles City records conceals the transfer of this title by Tucker & Company, but it appears (Hening, iii, 538; *Va. Mag.,* xxxi, 180) that the third Benjamin Harrison (who was speaker in 1705 and died in 1710) acquired Berkeley and established there the residence which has ever since been associated with his family name. This acquisition might be a clew to the still unproven identity of either the mother or the grandmother of this Benjamin Harrison. Was one of them a Tucker or a Thompson?

64. *Cal. Am. & W. I.,* 1706-08, pp. 205, 207; *W. & M. Quar.,* 2d Series, iii, 137.

65. *Spotswood Letters,* ii, 269.

66. *Patents,* 10 : 290. This, the grant of Germanna, was the first treasury right patent issued after the repeal of the act of 1705 (Hening, iii, 304). The form of the recital is, however, identical with that of the treasury right form set out in the act of 1705. The record abbreviates the formal clauses, as indicated in the transcript,

but it appears from later treasury right patents, which are recorded *in extenso* (e. g., *Patents*, 19: 997) that these clauses were identical with those of Spotswood's head right form, which has been quoted.

67. *Patents*, 1: 369. For the patentee, John Chew, see *Va. Mag.*, v, 341.

68. Hening, i, 326. For the construction of the forts and the indian treaty of 1646, see *ibid.*, i, 293, 315, 323.

69. *Patents*, 2: 195; 3: 13, 77. Apparently no patent was issued for Fort Charles at the falls of James River for the reason recited in the act of 1646, that there was no 'plantable land' adjoining it. In consideration of this fact the fort buildings were offered, either for their timber or to be burned to salvage the nails they contained, to whomever, buying out the rights of Capt. Thomas Harris who had commanded that fort, would seat a plantation on the South side of the river opposite the fort.

70. Hening, iii, 204. This interesting act was formulated in the interval between 'King William's War' and 'Queen Anne's War' against the French. The Virginia Assembly had refused to contribute a 'quota' to the defence of New York against Canada, and was loath to increase its levy for any purpose. Impressed, however, by Governor Nicholson's vigorous representations that the French were winning over the Iroquois and that if they denounced their English treaties there were familiar backwoods paths leading South from New York by which the Iroquois might be expected quickly and effectively to attack the undefended Virginia frontier, the Assembly proposed this act as a cheap measure of self-defence. It will be noted that one of the weapons described for the Virginia frontiersman was a 'sharp simeter.' This was the 'long knife.' The Iroquois name for the Governor of Virginia was 'Assarigoe,' which, said Philip Livingston in 1722, 'Signifys a Simeter or Cutlas which was given to Lord Howard, anno 1684, from the Dutch word *Hower*, a Cutlas.'

71. The Orders in Council are in Brock, *The Huguenot Emigration to Virginia* (Collections Va. Hist. Soc., N. S., vol. 5), but the Land Books do not show that a comprehensive patent was ever issued.

72. *Va. Mag.*, xxix, 14; *Acts*, P. C., Colonial, ii, p. 608; *Spotswood Letters*, i, 152. The language of the Lords of Trade, August 22, 1709, recommending a grant to Graffenried is significant: 'Wee pray your Lordship to represent to Her Majesty our humble opinion that the settlement of such a colony in the place desired [i. e-, on the Southwest Branch of Potomac] will be a publique benefit and Advantage by strengthening the Frontier of Virginia against the French of Canada and Mississippi.' With this *cf.* Sir William Keith's opinion in 1731 in support of the petition of Gould and Stauber for leave to establish another Swiss colony in the Shenandoah Valley (*Va. Mag.*, xxix, 183, 287). The failure of both these proposals was due to the uncertainty as to the boundaries of the proprietaries of the Northern Neck, Maryland and Pennsylvania.

73. Hening, iv, 77.

74. Council Journal, June 17, 1730, in *Va. Mag.*, xiii, 115.

75. For the Greenbrier and Loyal Companies see 4 Call, 21, and

Mr. B. W. Leigh's notes in *Code* 1819, ii, 347. In *Va. Mag.*, v, 173, 241, is an official list of 34 Orders in Council for similar frontier grants, made between 1745 to 1753. The motive of them all was the protection of the colony against the French and indians.

76. Hening, vi, 417.

77. *Dinwiddie Papers*, i, 90.

78. Hening, vii, 661.

79. *Patents*, 41 : 66.

80. *Acts, P. C.*, Colonial, iv, 573; *Virginia Gazette*, January 7, 1764; Hening, vii, 663.

81. *Va. Mag.*, v, 242. The treaty of Fort Stanwix is printed in *Va. Mag.*, xiii, 23.

82. *Patents*, 42 : 505. This patent has the interest of creating the first title to the site of the city of Louisville, now Kentucky.

83. For Virginia's recognition of Charles II in 1649 see *W. & M. Quar.*, i, 189; Hening, i, 360; *Va. Mag.*, i, 75; Clarendon, *Rebellion*, vi, 610. Although Charles II was proclaimed also in Scotland and Ireland by his adherents, in Virginia and Barbadoes an orderly government was carried on in his name.

84. The original charter of September 18, 1649, survives in the British Museum as *Add. Charter*, 13585. The patentees were therein recited as 'Ralph, Lord Hopton, Baron of Stratton; Henry Lord Jermyn, Baron of St. Edmund's Bury; John Lord Culpeper, Baron of Thoresway; Sir John Barkeley, Sir William Morton, Sir Dudley Wyatt & Thomas Culpeper, Esqr.' The parts they severally played in the Civil wars are writ large in Clarendon's pages, except in respect to Thomas Culpeper, whose military record may be found in Matthew Carter's *True Relation* of the siege of Colchester, 1648. After the Restoration Lord Jermyn became earl of St. Albans, and Sir John Berkeley, Baron Berkeley of Stratton.

One of the clichés of the 'republican' school of Virginia history is a sneer at the origin of the Northern Neck proprietary. The most casual comment on that institution has almost invariably dragged in a contemptuous arraignment of the 'questionable title' to a quarter of the colony, which Charles II vested in 'unworthy favorites.' Disregarding the fact that the charter antedated the era of favorites, and that, whatever some of them became later, in 1649 the grantees were not even courtiers, but champions of the Crown, most of whom had made masculine reputations on the battlefield (so that there was precisely the same consideration for their grant as there was later for George Washington's grant of his Kenawha lands, i. e., past military services), this sentiment has blossomed sometimes into salacious, but unexplained, inuendo like Paul Leicester Ford's reference (*True George Washington*, p. 210) to the Northern Neck charter as obtained 'from the Merrie Monarch by means so disreputable that they are best left unstated,' and sometimes into more comprehensible eloquence· 'In disregard of all valid land-titles and all valuable improvements upon the lands,' says Professor Moses Coit Tyler (*History of American Literature*, i, 70), 'the King kept giving away to his favorites large tracts of the most populous territory in Virginia, ignoring the real owners of the soil or transferring them

with it, as if they had been but herds of cattle or gangs of serfs.'
The uncritical acerbity of these writers seems to be actuated by
confusion of the Northern Neck grant of 1649 with Charles II's
subsequent grant in 1673, of all Virginia to Lords Arlington and
Culpeper. This later charter had its origin under conditions which
varied widely from those of 1649. As to the Northern Neck charter it
is sufficient for the purpose of this note to cite a sane observation upon it
by John Marshall. In reply to criticism similar to that to which reference has here been made, he said to the Court of Appeals of
Virginia in 1786 (*Hite* v. *Fairfax*, 4 Call at p. 69), 'Gentlemen cannot
suppose that a grant made by the Crown to the ancestor for services
rendered, or even for affection, can be invalidated in the hands of
the heir, because those services and that affection are forgotten . . .
it matters not whether the gentlemen themselves, or any others, would
or would not have made the grant or may now think proper to de-
nounce it as an unwise or unpolitic measure.'

85. For the slender testimonies of Sir Dudley Wyatt and Thomas
Culpeper in Virginia see *W. & M. Quar.*, x, 274; and the present
editor's genealogical study of the Culpepers.

86. See Charles II's letter to Governor Berkeley, December 5, 1662,
and August 3, 1663 (*Cal. Am. & W. I.*, 1661-68, No. 391, p. 116;
No. 520, p. 151).

87. *Acts P. C.*, Colonial, i, 373; *Cal. Am. & W. I.*, 1661-68, No.
1513, p. 476; Close Roll 4270 (21 Car. II, pt. 7), No. 10; Patent
Roll 21 Car. II, pt. 4, No. 6; *Cal. Am. & W. I.*, 1669-74, p. 22.

88. The Land Patent Books show the issue of seventeen patents
for Northern Neck lands between 1670 and 1679, but most of them
prove to be re-issues in the names of assignees of original patents
of the Commonwealth period. The notable exception is the patent
of December 29, 1677 (*Patents*, 6: 663), issued by Col. Herbert Jeffreys to Cadwallader and David Jones for 14114 acres on Acco-
tink and Pohick in Stafford. So far as the surviving record goes
this seems to be a new patent, but it may have been a confirmation
of a survey entered prior to 1669. In any event, as it is dated after
Lord Culpeper qualified as Governor, it must have been authorized
before his official caveat against the issue of further patents for
Northern Neck lands reached the colony. The minutes of the Council
which would give the explanation are missing.

89. The Arlington charter is printed in Hening, ii, 569. The reader
of the literature to which this grant gave rise will do well to re-
member that the controversy over it was ultimately pleaded to a
special issue. As shown by Francis Moryson's reports in 1675 (printed
by Burk), Virginia did not ever 'dispute his majesty's right to the
quit rents of that colony, nor his pleasure in transferring them;'
her consistent objection was to the exercise by 'particular persons'
of such 'regalities' within her territory as had been granted to Arlington. In this respect she stood on Charles I's declaration in 1626
that 'Virginia shall have no other dependence but only upon the Crown
of England.' Appreciating the force of this, Arlington declared that
the purpose of the regalities was 'only for the security of the quit
rents and escheats.' Thus in the end the question left for debate
was the rate at which Arlington was to accept tobacco in payment
of the quit rents.

90. Burk, ii, App. p. xxxv. This was one of the 'heads' of the statement by the Virginia Council to Lord Arlington in September, 1674. That it expressed Berkeley's own sentiments see his letter introducing the Virginia Commissioners to Arlington, and, more especially, his private protest to Lord Danby in a letter of February 1, 1675/6, which survives among the Duke of Leeds' papers and is calendared in Historical MSS. Commission *Report*, xi, Appendix 7, p. 10 (*Va. Mag.*, xxxii, 190).

91. *Cal. Am. & W. I.*, 1669-74, Nos. 145, 146, p. 53.

92. *Va. Mag.*, viii, 407; ix, 45.

93. *Journals H. B.*, 1660-98, p. 61.

94. Hening, ii, 311; Burk, ii, App. p. liv.

95. For Culpeper as a member of the Council of Foreign Plantations see *Cal. Am. & W. I.*, 1669-74, Nos. 470, 923, 943; for his interest in the charter of February, 1672/3, Hening, ii, 569; for the warrant dated June 19, 1675, for a patent to Culpeper as Governor of Virginia 'during life, immediately after the death, surrender or forfeiture of Sir William Berkeley,' *Cal. Am. & W. I.*, 1675-76, No. 599; 1677-80, No. 308; for the statement by the proprietors of the Northern Neck in 1676 of their previous recognition of Culpeper and Alexander Culpeper as each vested with a one-sixth interest in the Northern Neck charter of 1669, Burk, *History of Virginia*, ii, App. p., liv.

96. *N. N.*, 5: 207. First recorded in Stafford in March, 1690/1, as shown by the certificate endorsed on the original, this grant was recorded also in the Northern Neck Grant Books in April, 1719, while Edmund Jenings were agent. For the previous Lee title see *Landmarks of Old Prince William*, Chapter Three.

97. *Anthony Trethewy*, who here signs with Lord Culpeper, is recited in the deed of July 21, 1681 (by which Lord Culpeper acquired the other interests in the Northern Neck proprietary) to be the 'brother and assignee of John Trethewy, late of Datchett in the County of Somerset, Esq., deceased;' and it appears from the second Northern Neck charter (that of May 8, 1669) that John Trethewy 'had acquired Lord Hopton's interest in the proprietary, by purchase.
Reference must be had to the proprietors' 'common seal,' for contemporary evidence as to who those proprietors were in 1675. That seal, which survives on the original instrument now hanging framed in the hall at Mt. Vernon, is a marshalling of arms, viz: Quarterly, (1) Jermyn (2) Culpeper (3) Culpeper (4) Berkeley, charged with an escutcheon of pretense, the whole cinctured by the Garter of the earl of St. Albans and surmounted by his coronet. The escutcheon is, unfortunately, not certainly legible, but seems to be an impalement of the arms of Morton and Trethewy.

98. *Cal. Am. & W. I.*, 1677-80, No. 360. Herbert Jeffreys had been commissioned *Lieutenant* Governor on November 7, 1676, and took over the responsibility on the departure of Berkeley for England in the spring of 1677 (*ibid.*, 1675-76, No. 1118). He died on December 30, 1678 (*ibid.*, 1677-80, Nos. 758, 878) when Sir Henry Chicheley assumed the government under a commission as *Deputy* Governor which had been issued to him in 1674 (*ibid.*, 1669-74, No. 1228; 1677-80, No. 951). Accordingly, Jeffreys and Chicheley successively represented Culpeper until he arrived in the colony in May,

1680, and Chicheley carried on again during Culpeper's absence from August, 1680, to December, 1682. Chicheley died February 5, 1682/3, during Culpeper's second visit, and in consequence when the Governor departed in May, 1683, he left Secretary Nicholas Spencer in charge as President of the Council.

99. The deed from the other proprietors of the Northern Neck to Culpeper is in *Close Roll* 4568 (33 Car. II, part 14), No. 19. The Arlington deed is printed in Hening, ii, 578 from the subsequently lost *General Court D. B.*, 1682-89, No. 3, p. 28.

100. There are surviving testimonies for two of these 'Receivers General,' David Fox in Lancaster (*Lancaster W. & D.*, vi, 25), and George Brent in Stafford (*Va. Mag.*, ix, 309; *cf.* Fitzhugh in *ibid.*, i, 125). That they succeeded in collecting quit rents for Culpeper's account appears from a suit by the proprietor in Northumberland in May, 1682 (*Northumberland O. B.*, 1678-98, p. 129) on a protested bill of exchange which had been delivered in payment of quit rents.

101. *Close Roll* 4615 (36 Car. II, part 1), No. 16.

102. *Journals H. B.*, 1660-93, pp. 202, 203; printed also in Hening, iii, 26.

103. C. O., 5: 1324, p. 157.

104. *The Value of the Northern Neck proprietary*: When, following the American Revolution, Virginia undertook to forfeit the Northern Neck proprietary, the Assembly directed (Hening, xii, 111) the seizure of the 'records, documents, books and papers [in the proprietary office at Greenway Court] upon which the titles to their lands of the citizens of this Commonwealth depend.' It appears, from the memorial subsequently filed with the Commission on American Loyalist Claims by Robert, Lord Fairfax (P. R. O. Audit Office, 13: 28), that the authorities of the Commonwealth took possession also of papers which properly belonged to the proprietor's heirs, among others all 'papers of account relative to the said Estates.' While the grant books were deposited in the Land Office at Richmond and have survived, none of the other papers so confiscated is now to be found, and it seems likely that they were included among the colonial records which were burned with the General Court Office building in 1865. As a consequence of this loss no Northern Neck quit rent roll is now available on which conclusively to state the value of the proprietary at any period after 1732. There is, however, some secondary evidence. In the memorial of 1786 cited above, Robert, Lord Fairfax, alleged that when he was in Virginia in 1768 quit rents were collected by his brother at the rate of from £3,500 to £4,000 per annum, 'and were then in a regular course of increase as further grants or Dispositions of Land should be made.' On this basis the British government then calculated the capital value of the proprietary at £98,000 (Wilmot, *Historical View*, 1815). Colour is given to these estimates by the inventory of the sixth Lord Fairfax's personal estate at Greenway Court, taken in 1781, immediately after his death (*Va. Mag.*, viii, 11), which included an item of 'Cash in specie and paper currency £47,337, 3s., 9d.'

With these figures may be compared the capital valuation of £2,400 and the annuity of £300 per annum which the proprietors in 1675 and the fifth Lord Fairfax in 1708 were respectively willing to accept for a surrender of the charter (Burk, ii, Appendix, p. liv; *Acts P. C.*,

Colonial, vi, 95) ; and the net rental of £450 per annum which the sixth Lord Fairfax accepted from Robert Carter from 1722 to 1732 (C. O., 5: 1322, p. 103).

105. *Patent Roll*, 4 Jac. II, pt. 7, No. 2. This charter is printed, from the Randolph MS., in *Va. Mag.*, xv, 392. In the Harvard College Library there is an example of a contemporary print of the 'Septima pars.' Another such example (erroneously described in the catalogue as 'Culpeper Grant 1673') was included in the sale of the library of Judge Russell Benedict in New York in February, 1922.

106. *The waiver of the Proprietary claim to advowsons*: In 1736 the vestry of Truro recommended Dr. Charles Green to Lord Fairfax to be presented to the Bishop of London for ordination, promising to induct him into the living when so qualified. The Bishop duly ordained, but instead of collating Dr. Green immediately, the proprietor sent him to Governor Gooch who in turn presented him to the vestry: and Green was inducted in August, 1737 (*Truro Vestry Book*, ed. Goodwin, pp. 10, 13). It is recited in the minutes of the meeting of the Council on October 26, 1737, that 'upon his presenting the said Letter [Parson Green] behaved himself in a very unbecoming manner, as appears by two of the Vestry of the said Parish;' wherefore he was cited to appear before the Council. This he did on December 15th following, when the minutes noted that, being charged with 'speaking disrespectfully of the Governor's recommendation to the Vestry of Truro Parish' he acknowledged 'his error in insisting upon the Lord Fairfax's Right of presentation to the said parish, being so persuaded by his Lordship and not out of any disrespect to the Governor, to whom, he now understands, the right of such presentations is entrusted by his Majesties Instructions and the Law of the Colony . . . . Promising a more decent regard to the Laws and Constitution of this Colony for the future, he was thereupon dismissed.' On May 13, 1738 (*Fulham MS.*, Va., No. 191) Gooch wrote to Bishop Gibson: 'I have given Mr. Green notice that Your Lordship is satisfied with his settlement. Lord Fairfax very industriously gott that Gentleman recommended to Your Lordship without my knowledge, from an opinion he had of a Right to Collate to the vacant parishes in his Territory: but by his Lordship's sending Mr. Green to me upon his return to receive his appointment I concluded his Lordship had been better advised.' Thereafter the Governor regularly presented in the Northern Neck, as elsewhere; but it is interesting that with the characteristic phlegm which was part of his inheritance from his Dutch grandmother Lord Fairfax undertook to make disposition in his will of 'the several advowsons, and the rights of presentation thereto belonging or appertaining, I have' in the Northern Neck.

107. For the English usage see the examples from the seventeenth century and later, quoted in the Oxford Dictionary under 'Head, sb. 16.' The Virginia usage is well illustrated in the acts of 1676 and 1679 (Hening, ii, 327, 433), providing for construction of forts at the heads of all the great rivers, and specifying sites which in every case were below the falls. Undoubtedly Culpeper had these acts in mind when the charter of 1688 was drafted.

108. The sordid facts about Lord Culpeper's death and the settlement of his estate are collected in the present editor's genealogical study, *The Proprietors of the Northern Neck*.

109. The first appearance of Lord Fairfax on the Northern Neck record was when he joined his wife, Lady Culpeper and Alexander Culpeper in the petition to the Crown for confirmation of the charter of 1688. This petition was dated May 21, 1691 (*Acts P. C.*, Colonial, ii, 188).

110. *Cal. Am. & W. I.*, 1689-92, No. 1003.

111. *Va. Mag.*, ix, 32.

112. *Journals H. B.*, 1660-93, p. 371.

113. *Acts P. C.*, Colonial, ii, 188; *Cal. Am. & W. I.*, 1689-92, No. 1514; 1693-94, No. 34.

114. Every investigator in the field of Virginia history has had occasion to lament the burning of the General Court office building, with most of the ancient records it contained, at the evacuation of Richmond by the Confederacy in April, 1865 (See Mr. Brock's notes in Winsor, *Narr. and Crit. History*, iii, 127; reprinted in *Collections, Va. Hist. Society*, vii, at p. xxiv). The General Court kept record books of Deeds, Wills, Bonds, etc., which were of larger import than any one county and in these books were recorded some, if not all, the powers of attorney of the agents of the proprietors of the Northern Neck and other general papers relating to that special jurisdiction. Thanks to the industry of Messrs. Burk and Hening at the beginning of the nineteenth century, a few papers vital to the present study were extracted from these books and printed; and Mr. Conway Robinson left MS. notes of his later reading in the same records, which have been printed in *Va. Mag.*, viii, 64 ff (where see Dr. Stanard's comment in the neglect of these records by the historian while they were still extant). So far as they go, such vestiges are invaluable, but they serve also to bring some appreciation of what is now lost.

The records of the older Northern Neck counties are practically bare of instruments relating to the proprietary. Careful and systematic search of the most complete of those records, those of Northumberland, Lancaster and Westmoreland, made on behalf of the present editor, has demonstrated this conclusively. This is not surprising in view of the hostility of the Virginia government to the proceedings of the earliest Northern Neck agents. Indeed, in 1690, by order of the Council, Governor Nicholson issued a proclamation specifically instructing every County Court north of the Rappahannock to deny record to proprietary papers, and to return to Jamestown all those which previously had been recorded. This was duly done (See *Northumberland O. B.*, 1678-98, pp. 530, 544; *Lancaster O. B.*, 1686-90, p. 781; *Westmoreland O. B.*, 1690-98, p. 10).

115. *Cal. Am & W. I.*, 1661-68, Nos. 391, 520; 1669-74, No. 145.

116. For Thomas Kirton in Virginia, see Conway Robinson's notes from the Council Journal, *Va. Mag.*, viii, 407, iv, 45; the recitals in *N. N.*, 1: 160, 2: 14; *Northumberland O. B.*, 1666-78, p. 77; *Westmoreland O. B.*, 1676-89. For the Kirton family see the pedigree in F. A. Crisp, *Somersetshire Wills* (1887), i, 44; where a Thomas Kirton appears as the youngest of six children named in the will (proved 1620, P. C. C. *Soame*, 98) of their uncle Sir James Kirton of Almesford.

Dr. Tyler notes (*W. & M. Quar.*, iv, 38; vi, 224) that Kirton married the widow of that picturesque worthy, 'Dick' Cole of Westmoreland, and died in Virginia in 1678. If so, he must have left a son, for a Thomas Kirton contracted with the Westmoreland Court in November, 1686, to transcribe all the records of that county 'into one book;' (*Westmoreland O. B.*, 1676-89, p. 529) and in 1690 had a land grant on the Occoquan, which he conveyed to Isaac Allerton in January, 1691/2 (*N. N.*, 1: 45; *Westmoreland W. & D.*, ii, 13). It was probably this younger Kirton who appears in Westmoreland Court in June, 1677, as 'collector of his Majesty's quit rents.'

117. *N. N.*, 5: 207. Diligent search has failed to find any mention of Aretkin in the surviving county records, but this may probably be explained by his residence in Stafford, of which the records in his time are lost.

118. Conway Robinson's notes in *Va. Mag.*, ix, 306.

119. *Daniel Parke, Senior* (1629-1679) was of an Essex family and was bred to trade in London. He established himself in Virginia in 1651, became a justice of York County in 1655, burgess, 1660-1670, was raised to the Council in 1670, and succeeded Thomas Ludwell as Secretary of State in 1678. According to a modern MI. in Bruton Church at Williamsburg, he died March 6, 1679. This means 1678/9, for his will (P. C. C. *King*, 120; calendared in *Va. Mag.*, xiv, 174) was proved September 16, 1679.

120. *Nicholas Spencer* (1633-1689) was a younger son of a Bedfordshire squire, according to Beverley a cousin to the Culpepers, but how is not suggested by the Visitation of Beds of 1634 in which his name is listed. His first appearance in relation to Virginia is in 1659, when he is recited in a business paper as 'of London, merchant.' He seems to have emigrated about this time, and there acquired the lands at the head of Nomini River in Westmoreland, which were later called for him 'the Secretary's Neck,' and which Robert Carter in turn acquired from his estate in 1707 and vested in his second son. Spencer entered public life in Virginia as a burgess for Westmoreland in 1666, served as Naval Officer for Potomac River, and in 1671 was advanced to the Council. In 1678 he became Secretary of State and in 1683, being then by seniority President of the Council, acted as Governor after Culpeper's final departure from the colony. For his pedigree see *Va. Mag.*, ii, 32; his will, proved in London ten years after his death, is P. C. C. *Noel*, 14, calendared in Waters' *Gleanings*, i, 492. He married a daughter of John Mottrom of Northumberland and his descendants are recited in *Va. Mag.*, iv, 451. A great mass of Spencer's official letters, ranging from 1673-1689, survive in the Public Record Office, many of which are calendared in the Am. & W. I. series.

121. *Philip Ludwell* (1638?-1723) came of the family of that name which had its origin at Bruton in Somersetshire and was connected by blood with the Berkeleys. He emigrated to Virginia after the Restoration and began his career there as deputy for his elder brother, Thomas, the Secretary of State under Sir William Berkeley. For his subsequently highly coloured Virginia record see *Va. Mag.*, i, 174; for his service in Carolina, Hawks' *History of N. C.*, ii, 492; Rivers' *Historical Collections S. C.*, p. 159. He was superseded as Governor of Carolina in August, 1694, and returned to Virginia, where he served

as Speaker at the session of the Assembly in April, 1695 (*Cal. Am. & W. I.*, 1693-96, p. 462). In 1700 he returned to England and there spent the remainder of his life in retirement. In a letter of July 10, 1711, to his son in Virginia, an English correspondent mentions him as 'the old gentleman' (*Va. Mag.*, iv, 19) and in another such letter, of January 4, 1723/4, Thomas Ludwell of Bruton says: 'I have put on five mourning rings in memory of your good father' (*Va. Mag.*, iii, 354). This would indicate that he lived into his eighty-sixth year. Persistent search of the English records has, however, failed to discover either his will, if any, or any testimony by parish register or tombstone to vouch for the date of his death.

122. *Cal. Am. & W. I.*, 1689-92, No. 1154.

123. *Cal. Am. & W. I.*, 1689-92, No. 1132.

124. *Westmoreland O. B.*, 1690-98, p. 10. *Cf. Westmoreland W. & D.*, v, 63, for a later recital that Ludwell's office was in Westmoreland·

125. For the local significance of the Nomini neighbourhood see *post,* n. 172.

126. *Richard Whitehead* lived in Abingdon parish of Gloucester (*W. & M. Quar.*, xvii, 300; *Journals H. B.*, 1659-95, p. 254). The loss of the records of that county has left him, like many other Gloucestershire worthies, something of a shadow. Piecing out some random notes collected in other relations (*W. & M. Quar.*, iv, 90; vii, 86; *Va. Mag.*, i, 241; v, 67; xi, 67; xiii, 200) one gathers that he was a surveyor by profession and as early as 1673 was associated with Philip Ludwell in land speculation on the Mattaponi River in that part of New Kent which ultimately became King William and Caroline. He was reported to have suffered in Bacon's Rebellion 'by plundering and in person' and in 1684 was one of the jury which tried the plant cutters. The recitals of *N. N.*, 2: 14, confirm that set out in the text that he was Ludwell's deputy in the Northern Neck from 1690 to 1693. After Brent and Fitzhugh discharged him from this employment he was Surveyor of King and Queen. In 1695 in a slander suit he recited that he 'hath been imployed, invested with and put into, places and offices of great Trust . . . by the approbation of worthy and Honᵇˡᵉ persons of this colony.' He had a wife with the curious name Damazina and it is probable that the Philip Whitehead of King William who, in 1705, was one of the founders of Delawaretown (West Point) was his son, named for Philip Ludwell.

127. For Francis Wright see *Tyler's Quar.*, iv, 164.

128. *Va. Mag.*, iv, 184.

129. The records of Northumberland, Lancaster and Westmoreland have been searched in vain for a transcript of Ludwell's procuration. It may well have been one of the papers filed for record in Westmoreland and subsequently remitted to Jamestown. The quotation of its tenor is Ludwell's own recitation in his grants.

130. *N. N.*, 1: 4.

131. *George Brent* (1630?-1699) came of a Catholic family of Somersetshire, one of whom married a Culpeper before 1557. His uncle, Giles Brent, had played a large part in the colonization of Maryland

and about 1648 quit that province, crossed the Potomac, and established himself in the Virginia wilderness on the point above Potomac Creek, where he dubbed his house 'Peace.' Hither George emigrated direct from England about 1650 and seated himself on Aquia on the lands since known as 'Woodstock.' Although a steadfast Catholic in a self-consciously protestant community, during the remainder of his life he was a prominent figure on the Potomac frontier, as surveyor, lawyer, captain of militia, and large landholder. Nicholas Spencer appointed him an executor, with the description 'my singular good friend.' His name remains on the map in 'Brentsville,' sometime the county seat of Prince William. The surviving fragment of his will is printed in *Va. Mag.*, xviii, 96. The relations of his descendants to 'Brent Town' are rehearsed in *Tyler's Quar.*, iv, 164.

132. *William Fitzhugh* (1651-1700) of 'Bedford' (originally in Stafford but now in King George) is one of the most clearly defined figures in the colonial annals of Virginia by reason of the fortunate preservation of his letter book, which is printed in *Va. Mag.*, i-vi. He emigrated to Virginia about 1670 (*Va. Mag.*, vii, 198) and named his seat on the Potomac for his native shire in England, being thus a countryman of Nicholas Spencer. For a living picture of a Christmas frolic at 'Bedford' in 1686 see the memoirs of the Huguenot Durand, translated (1924) as *A Frenchman in Virginia*.

133. *Va. Mag.*, iv, 183. *Roger Jones* came to Virginia 'a soldier under Lord Culpeper and was by him made captain of a small sloop which was manned to carry twelve men and cruise in prevention of illicit traders' (See Nicholson's dispatch of July 6, 1692, in *Cal. Am. & W. I.*, 1689-92, No. 2318, p. 665; and for the sloop, *Katherine, ibid.*, 1681-85, p. 443). In the course of this cruising Jones was entertained at Bedford and in January, 1682/3, was on such a footing of intimacy with Fitzhugh that the latter bespoke his influence with Lord Culpeper (*Va. Mag.*, i, 116). Jones ultimately established himself as a merchant in London, where he lived until 1702, maintaining with Lord Culpeper's family relations of confidence. Several of his descendants have distinguished themselves in the military service of the United States. See L. H. Jones, *The Descendants of Capt. Roger Jones*, Louisville, Kentucky, 1871.

134. Brent was 'Receiver General' for Stafford by Culpeper's appointment in 1683 and the certificate of record of the Brent Town grant of 1687 recites Fitzhugh as 'attorney of the within named Thomas Lord Culpeper.'

135. See Fitzhugh's offers to farm portions of the proprietary in *Va. Mag.*, i, 125; ii, 273, 370.

136. See Chapter Three.

137. *Cal. Am. & W. I.*, 1693-96, No. 1871. This dispatch was an acknowledgment of the instructions of November 30, 1694, to support Brent and Fitzhugh and an excuse for the failure to do so.

138. The quotation is from the recital of the Brent and Fitzhugh procuration in that of 1702 to Robert Carter, cited in note 144.

139. *N. N.*, 2: 14.

140. P. C. C. *Irby*, 3.

141. Beginning in January, 1695, the records in *N. N.,* 2 abbreviate the recital of the proprietors as 'Margarett Lady Culpeper, Thomas Lord Fairfax &c' and thus afford no evidence as to when, if ever, Brent and Fitzhugh took notice of the death of Alexander Culpeper.

142. There are several interesting contemporary testimonies of the importance of the mercantile house of Perry and Lane with reference to the American colonies during the first half of the eighteenth century. See, *e. g.,* Mr. Austin Dobson's discussion (*Eighteenth Century Vignettes,* Third Series) of the dedication to them of James Puckle's Book *The Club,* first published in 1711 and long a 'best seller ;' and compare Spotswood's comment (*Spotswood Letters,* ii, 79) on 'old Perry' in 1714: 'It is doing little honour to the Government to have its Council appointed in the Virginia Coffee House, and I believe a Governor who has a power under the Great Seal . . . is as capable of Judging of the qualification requisite for Persons in that Post as any Merchant in London who has no other rule to judge of a man's merit than by the Number of his Tobacco hogsheads.' This first Micajah Perry died in 1721 (See his will proved October 3, 1721, P. C. C. *Buckingham,* 185) leaving his Virginia business to his grandson of the same name, who was an Alderman of London, 1728-1746, served the office of Sheriff (1734) and Lord Mayor (1738-39) ; and sat as M. P. for the City of London, 1727-1734, and 1741 (Beaven's *Aldermen of London,* i, 14, 257, 279, 280, 292, 320; ii, 127, 196). This second Micajah Perry, who also appears frequently in Virginia records, died January 22, 1753 (P. C. C. *Admon Act Book,* August 14, 1753).

143. *Robert Carter* (1663-1732), son of a planter who had greatly prospered but whose origin has not yet been proved (See Keith, *Ancestry of Benjamin Harrison*), was born in Virginia, where he lived out his life except for the years of boyhood spent in England at school. He ran the whole colonial *cursus honorum.* Burgess for Lancaster in 1691, Speaker in 1696 and 1699, he was raised to the Council in that latter year and eventually by seniority became President, so that he had the opportunity to be acting Governor in the interval between the death of Governor Drysdale and the arrival of Gooch. See his portrait and extraordinary MI. in *Va. Mag.,* xxxii, 18. His familiar sobriquet was in use as early as 1704. When Governor Nicholson quarrelled with him in that year he recorded a 'character' of Carter (*Va. Mag.,* viii, 56) in which he animadverted upon 'his extraordinary Pride and Ambition, his using people haughtily, sometimes making the Justices of the Peace of the county wait two or three hours before they can speak to him . . . To people that will flatter, cajole and as it were adore him, he is familiar enough, but others he uses with all the haughtiness and insolence possible. In contempt of him he is sometimes called King Carter and other times Robin Carter, even to his face.'

144. *Westmoreland D. B.,* 3: 95, 112. This, the first of the agents' procurations of which a complete transcript survives, seems to owe that fortune to the fact that on December 4, 1702, Carter deputed Daniel Tebbs of Westmoreland to collect the proprietary dues in that county, whereupon Tebbs got the county court to record together Carter's power and his own deputation in order to facilitate his work. This is the earliest record evidence that the local official ban upon the proprietary had been withdrawn.

145. *N. N.*, 3: 88. This particular grant is selected as an illustration because it originated the title to the site of the first Prince William court house· It was also the nucleus of the Mason estate later known as 'Woodbridge.'

146. *Cal. Treasury Papers*, 1708-14, p. 103; *Blathwayts Journal* (L. C. Transcripts), ii, 401; *Acts P. C.*, Colonial, vi, 95.

147. The probate of the fifth Lord Fairfax's will (P. C. C. *Young*, 45) gives the date of his death.

148. *Cf. N. N.*, 3: 257 and 261.

149. Bromfield parish register. Lady Culpeper's will is P. C. C. *Smith*, 145. The last recital of her as one of the proprietors in *N. N.*, 4: 33, dated May 9, 1711.

150. *N. N.*, 4: 34, dated May 9, 1711, like the last proceeding grant, which recited Lady Culpeper as a party.

151. By *N. N.*, 4: 36, dated May 20, 1711. There are, however, a number of subsequent grants recorded in *N. N.*, 4: in which the blunder is repeated.

152. *The Fairfax Correspondence* (ed. Bell, 1849), iv, 242.

153. *Henry Corbin* (1629-1675) of a Warwickshire family, emigrated to Virginia in 1654, seated himself in that part of Lancaster which became Middlesex, and after service as a burgess was advanced to the Council in 1663 (*Lee of Virginia*, p. 84). His son, Thomas, born in Virginia, removed to London where he entered the counting house of an uncle, Gawin Corbin, and eventually succeeded to the business as a Virginia merchant (*Acts P. C.*, Colonial, ii, 492). One of Thomas's sisters married the second Richard Lee, and another, Edmund Jenings. The subsequent Virginia Corbins descended from a younger branch.

154. *Edmund Jenings* (1659-1727) was son of Sir Edmund Jenings, M. P. for Ripon, and later sheriff of Yorkshire (*Va. Mag.*, xii, 308). He was educated in the law and when he came of age (1680, see *Va. Mag.*, vi, 398) was sent out to Virginia with a commission as Attorney General, a post which his kinsman, Capt. Peter Jenings, had held in Berkeley's time. He was advanced to the Council in 1691 (*Acts P. C.*, Colonial, ii, 824) and in 1702 (*ibid.*, p. 368) was appointed Secretary of State in succession to Ralph Wormeley. His most important and most useful service in the colony was from 1704 to 1710, when, as President of the Council, he acted as Governor. No transcript of Jenings' procuration in respect to the Northern Neck has come to light.

155. *Westmoreland D. B.*, 5: 56. Thomas Lee (1690-1750), named for his uncle, Thomas Corbin, was the youngest son of the second Richard Lee of Westmoreland. He was left by his father's early death without the opportunity of the English education which his brothers enjoyed, but, nevertheless, by his native parts and industry surpassed them all. Incidentally, he begot six sons who were all large figures in the American Revolution (See *Lee of Virginia*, p. 103). He had contacts with the Northern Neck proprietors not only by inheritance and residence, but by marriage, for his wife was a granddaughter of the Philip Ludwell who was a proprietary agent before him. First returned as burgess for Westmoreland in 1720,

he was unseated on a contest by Daniel McCarty, but in 1727 established himself firmly in the Assembly and in 1733 was advanced to the Council (*Acts P. C.*, Colonial, iii, 839). He ended his life as President and acting Governor after the departure of Gooch.

156. Fairfax MSS., Bodleian Library, Oxford.

157. *N. N.*, 5: 1. Lee appended the following note to this record, viz: 'This is the first deed granted by virtue of power from the Lady Fairfax, sole proprietor of the Northern Neck of Virginia, dated December 7, 1711, and published and recorded in the General Court and County Court after I had another more full power proved in Gloucester Court.' No 'more full power' is recorded in any of the Northern Neck counties, and the loss of the Gloucester records has destroyed the evidence to which Lee refers, and with it the explanation of what Lee was doing in Gloucester Court.

The last recorded grant by Lee is recorded March 17, 1715/16 (*N. N.*, 5: 126).

158. Jenings signed his first grant under date December 21, 1715, but he did not begin to sign all grants until December 7, 1716 (*N. N.*, 5: 128). His last grant before closing the land office upon receipt of news of Lady Fairfax's death, was one to Thomas Lee dated August 4, 1719 (*N. N.*, 5: 240). This grant is interesting not only because of its date, but because it included the future site of Fauquier Court House (Warrenton).

159. Bromfield parish register. Lady Fairfax's will is P. C. C. *Browning*, 105.

160. *William Cage*, sheriff of Kent in 1695 and M. P. in 1702, 1710 and 1713, was a grandson, by his first marriage, of that William Cage of Milgate in Bersted, who, in 1637, married secondly, Joan Culpeper, a sister of Lady Fairfax's grandmother; and in consequence is called 'brother' by the first Lord Culpeper in his will (Berry, *Kentish Genealogies*, p. 273; *Harl. Soc. Pubs.*, xxvi, 232; and the M. I. of Elizabeth, wife of Sir Thomas Culpeper, the elder, in Hollingbourne Church, Cave-Brown, p. 20); but he was of kin to Lady Fairfax because his mother was a daughter of her grandmother's brother, Sir Cheney Culpeper. Lady Fairfax had depended upon this 'cousin' for business advice for some time before she made her will. Thus in her letter to her son, December 15, 1711 (*The Fairfax Correspondence*, iv, 244) she says 'Colonial Cage is a great and entire friend to me, and you have reason to respect him.' When Fairfax went out to Virginia in 1747 he took with him one of this family. See the lively fox hunting letter of J. Cage, written from Belvoir to Capt. Lawrence Washington at Mt. Vernon, in Conway, *Barons*, p. 245.

161. *Edward Filmer* had been a practising barrister at the Parliamentary bar but was soon to become, on the death of his father in 1720, the third baronet on his house. Referring to him, Lord Fairfax wrote to George William Fairfax, April 6, 1747, just before his final departure from England (Neill, p. 77), 'I have sent you by Captain Cooling of the *Elizabeth* two dogs and one bitch of Sir Edward Filmer's hounds which he promised you.'

The Filmers of East Sutton were also of kin to the Wigsell Culpepers (*Cf.* the will of Samuel Filmer, 1670, P. C. C. *Penn.*, 58, calendared in *Va. Mag.*, xv, 181) through the St. Legers and the

Scotts, but they have their own claims to the interest of Virginians. They descend from that Samuel Argall who was one of the early Governors, and had maintained their relation with the colony. Thus, in 1643, Henry Filmer was a resident of Warwick County, serving as a burgess and justice of the County Court. He was a brother of the Sir Robert Filmer, author of the *Patriarcha* (*Dict. Nat. Biog.*, re-issue, vi, 1304) and a great great uncle of Lady Fairfax's trustee. For this family, see the Visitation of Kent, 1619, Berry, *Kent*, and *Va. Mag.*, xv, 181.

162. *Robert Carter's lease of the Northern Neck*: None of the county records in the Northern Neck affords any testimony for the instrument which defined the powers and conditions under which Robert Carter's second agency was conducted. That paper was undoubtedly recorded in the lost books of the General Court. That it was a lease appears, however, from the following evidences, viz: (a) the devise in Carter's will of 1726 (*Va. Mag.*, vi, 2) to his son, John, of 'the Lease I have lately taken and am now in possession of, of the Northern Neck from the proprietors;' (b) a comment in a letter from Carter to Cage, of which the surviving copy (*Carter Letter Book*, MS.) bears no date but which discusses the preparations for the attack on the proprietary which was precipitated in 1730 and so may be related to 1728: here Carter says, 'my lease wears out apace: it will be no great loss to me let it go as it will;' (c) Gooch's report to the Lords of Trade (C. O., 5: 1322, p. 103) in July, 1730, that the Northern Neck 'is now farmed by the Proprietors at £450 per annum and it is supposed to be worth £700, besides that 'tis still increasing by new Settlements;' (d) a reference in the *Autobiography* of John Page (*Va. Hist. Register*, iii, 144) to a tradition that Robert Carter 'held the high office of agent for the Proprietor of the Northern Neck by purchase from the Lord Proprietor, his friend (*sic*), who was contented (*sic*) to receive but £300 per annum for it (*sic*), as the report of the family stated.'

163. *N. N.*, A: 1.

164. The Bromfield parish register records the date of the sixth Lord Fairfax's birth in an entry, October 31, 1693, on the occasion of his baptism. The same record contains a similar contemporary entry of his death 'at his Proprietary in Virginia, 9 December, 1781, in the eighty-ninth year of his age.' It will be noted that he had only recently passed his eighty-eighth anniversary, and that Burnaby was in error in his often quoted statement that he died 'in the 92d year of his age.'

165. *Carter Letter Book*, MS., Virginia Historical Society.

166. *The forfeitures for crime*: Lord Fairfax's inheritance of this particular feudality throughout the Northern Neck was derived from a specific grant in the charter of 1688. The earlier charters of 1649 and 1669 had granted such forfeitures only as an incident to the judgment of a court-leet held in a manor erected within the proprietary. That incident was duly carried forward into the charter of 1688; but Lord Culpeper had seen the failure of Lord Baltimore's attempt to transfer to America the manor as that institution was practised in England, and with it the court-leet, and appreciated that under slave-holding conditions no such institution could ever be successfully established in Virginia. Knowing also the value of the for-

feitures as adjudged in the county courts, he had made provision accordingly when the charter of 1688 was drafted.

Robert Carter was apparently the first to make this feudality effective in the Northern Neck. His letter to Col. Cage of July 4, 1723 (*Carter Letter Book MS.*) and his will of 1726 (*Va. Mag.*, vi, 6), show that soon after his second agency began one Thomas Glascock was convicted of murder in Richmond County, whereupon Carter claimed Glascock's negroes and chattels as forfeited to the proprietor. The claim was disputed by the Crown officers, but Carter took possession of the property and by his will, reciting such possession in the right that it 'was forfeited to me as the proprietor's agent,' bequeathed the property to his eldest son. Later, in August, 1727, he secured an opinion from the Attorney General sustaining what he had done. Thenceforth the proprietor collected all forfeitures without opposition, as Dinwiddie testified in his annual report for 1755 (*Dinwiddie Papers*, i, 385).

167. *Journals H. B.*, 1727-40, p. 92. The editor of the Assembly Journal seems to regard this as a popular movement, but a study of the documents is persuasive that although the protest is given the popular form traditional to all legislative petitions, it was actuated, not by the residents of the Northern Neck, but by the patent officers at Williamsburg, who were seeking to protect their fees. While the petition dealt with the boundary, the gravamen of it was the charge that 'the Grant of Felons Goods, Fines and Forfeitures doth not only in many cases that may deserve compassion subject the people of this Territory to the Will and Avarice of the Proprietor but they are likewise as to these matters excluded from your Majesties Mercy and Clemency, which insupportable mischief must give occasion to continual Murmurings and Complaints of your people.'

This was the eloquent translation of what Robert Carter had heard that 'the Recvr Gen'l and the Commissary too, the Auditor's Uncle, give it as their clear opinion that the lands above Chenandoah undoubtedly belong'd to the Crown.' The clew to this statement is provided by William Beverley of Blandfield. In a letter to Lord Fairfax of May 18, 1739 (*W. & M. Quar.*, iii, 228), he said: 'I do verily believe the people [of the Northern Neck] would have been very easy from the beginning if they had not been stirred up by some persons who had private views of their own to carry out.'

168. There is a full calendar of the judicial proceedings from 1733 to 1745 for the ascertainment of the bounds of the Northern Neck, in *Acts P. C.*, Colonial, iii, 385, ff. This supplies facts and dates which have been vague in Virginia records, and should be read as a balance to Col. Byrd's picturesque brief of his side of the controversy, which is printed in *Westover MSS.*, ed. Wynne.

169. *Cal. Treasury Books and Papers*, 1731-34, pp. 398, 524. Here it appears also that the tentative appointment was duly confirmed on October 17, 1733, '*vice* Henry Moryson deceased.'

William Fairfax (1691-1757) was born in Yorkshire, son of a younger brother of the fifth Lord Fairfax. After a subaltern's career in the navy during the war of the Spanish Succession, he resigned in 1712 to embark in the colonial service. His preliminary essay was with 'John Company' in India. In 1718 he went to the Bahamas under Capt. Woodes Rogers, the first royal governor of those islands. There he played various parts in the government until 1729 [not 1725, as stated by Burnaby], when his friends at home got him the appointment as Collector of Customs at Salem in Massachusetts. In Virginia, in addition to his duties as Collector of Customs for the South Potomac and agent for the Northern Neck, he served as a Burgess for Prince William and Fairfax until, in 1743, he was advanced to the Council as the successor to old Commissary Blair. By seniority he succeeded as President of the Council at the beginning of Governor Dinwiddie's proconsulship. He married three times: (1) in India, a lady whose name is lost; (2) in the Bahamas, Sarah Walker; and (3) at Salem, Deborah Clarke; and left children by his last two wives, one of whom ultimately succeeded as the eighth Lord Fairfax. His will is printed in *Va. Mag.*, iv, 102. There is a pleasant, if not altogether accurate, account of William Fairfax in Archdeacon Burnaby's *Travels Through the Middle Settlements* (1798), but his best monuments consist of his surviving letters, some of which are printed in Neill, *The Fairfaxes of England and America* (1806) and others in Hamilton, *Letters to Washington*.

170. *Prince William D. B.*, B: 349.

171. H. F. Waters, from Salem records in *Historical Collections Essex Institute*, xvi (1880), 241.

172. *Westmoreland O. B.*, 1731-39, p. 148. It appears from the Council Journal that in 1732 Henry Moryson, who was William Fairfax's predecessor as Collector for South Potomac, maintained his custom house at Nomini and for that reason was included in the Westmoreland commission of the peace.

At this time Nomini Bay was the centre of the commercial life of the Potomac. Culpeper's act of 1680 (Hening, ii, 471; *Cf.*, iii, 60) had designated it as a town site and in 1730 Gooch's tobacco inspection act (Hening, iv, 267) emphasized this by making it the site of a warehouse. This commercial prestige was not due so much to preeminent natural advantages as to propinquity to the estates of a succession of political magnates who held the office of Naval Officer for the Potomac District. Nicholas Spencer, Robert Carter, Jr., and three Lees (the second Richard, Thomas, and the first Henry) all found Nomini a convenient place to collect Virginia duties, and for that reason persistently contrived to draw commerce thither.

173. The Council Journal on September 5, 1734 (C. O., 5: 1420, p. 60), includes an item, '*Ordered* that a new commission of the Peace be issued for the County of Westmoreland and that Wᵐ ffairfax, Esq., be added to the Quorum.' He did not, however, qualify as a Justice until July 29, 1735, but thenceforth he continued to sit in Westmoreland Court from time to time until April 1, 1741 (*Westmoreland O. B.*, 1731-39, p. 176; 1739-41, p. 91. See also *Cal. Va. State Papers*, i, 223, 225, 228, 232; *Journals H. B.*, 1727-40, p. 383). In Lord Fairfax's commission for the survey, which is dated September 13, 1736 (*Westover MSS.*, ed. Wynne, ii, 94), William Fairfax is described as 'of the County of Westmoreland, Esqr.'

174. For Lord Fairfax's arrival, see Gooch's dispatch, January 8, 1735/6 (C. O., 5: 1324, p. 69). His resort to Westmoreland is proven by his letters written thence, which are printed in *Cal. Va. State Papers*, i, 225.

175. *Journals H. B.*, 1727-40, pp. 295, 315; Hening, iv, 514. See also Gooch's dispatch of December 5, 1736, to the Lords of Trade, rehearsing the act and reporting that it was 'passed with Lord Fairfax's consent, who was with me when it made its progress.'

176. *Acts P. C.*, Colonial, iii, 853; where the record is annotated 'confirmed, Lord Fairfax having consented.'

177. As late as 1836 the Court of Appeals of Virginia (*Stephen v. Swann*, 9 Leigh, 404), struggling with the glosses of Lord Fairfax's will in the various judgments in the Hite case, was obliged to hold the act of 1736 'equivalent, I think, to an express patent or grant' by which Lord Fairfax 'has ever since been considered in our Courts as tenant in fee of the lands within the Northern Neck, having a property in the soil and a complete seisin and possession independent of his seignorial rights.'

178. *N. N.*, E: 1.

179. *N. N.*, E: 7. In addition to this testimony of the Grant Books, there is other evidence that William Fairfax removed his residence to King George in the spring of 1737 and there maintained the Northern Neck Land Office for more than two years. He was added to the commission of the peace in King George in March, 1736/7, and served thenceforth in that capacity until December, 1740 (*King George O. B.*, 1735-51, pp. 97, 245. See also *Journals H. B.*, 1727-40, p. 383). On June 15, 1739, William Beverley addressed a letter 'to William Fairfax, Esqr. at his house in King George' (*Cal. Va. State Papers*, i, 232). The King George records fail to show that William Fairfax acquired any lands in that county and it seems to follow that he lived in a rented house, probably one belonging to his friend, Charles Carter of Cleve. That this house was at Falmouth appears from the description of William Fairfax in several deeds, surviving in Prince William records and ranging in date from August 7, 1739, to January 27, 1740/1, as 'of Hanover parish, King George County.'

180. William Beverley's letters to Lord Fairfax from 1738 to 1742 (*W. & M. Quar.*, iii, 227) repeatedly refer to his expectation of the proprietor's return to Virginia as soon as he should secure the judgment of the Privy Council on the bounds of the Northern Neck.

181. This is Gooch's testimony in his dispatch of November 6, 1737 (*C. O.*, 5: 1324, p. 197). The date is borne out by the fact that Lord Fairfax signed his last grant on September 26, 1737 (*N. N.*, E: 38).

182. *Westmoreland Fiduciary Accounts*, No. 1: 240, recorded September 6, 1740.

183. In a deed dated November 10, 1741, William Fairfax was described as 'of the County of Prince William.' In April, 1741, he was named 'first' in a new commission of the peace for Prince William (*Va. Mag.*, xv, 114). It was at this time also that he withdrew from the Westmoreland and King George courts. The last grant which recites the office in King George is *N. N.*, E: 347, and the first which recites it in Prince William is *N. N.*, E: 348, both dated in October, 1741.

With a grant dated December 1, 1742 (*N. N.*, F: 30) the recital was changed to read 'in the county of Fairfax.' That county had been carved out of Prince William by the act (Hening, v, 207) which became law June 19, 1742, and included Belvoir.

184. *W. & M. Quar.*, iii, 231.

185. The order in Council of April 11, 1745 (calendared in *Acts P. C.*, Colonial, iii, 385) is here quoted from the transcript in C. O., ⟨5: 1326, p. 293. With it should be compared the bill passed by the Assembly on December 14, 1748 (*Journals H. B.*, 1742-49, p. 322; Hening, vi, 198), entitled 'An act for confirming the grants made by his majesty within the bounds of the Northern Neck as they are now established.' In view of the place this 'act' took in the subsequent jurisprudence of Virginia it should be noted that it was no more than a colonial minute of what had already been adjudged by the Privy Council. When the other acts of that session were under review by the Privy Council this chapter 55 was neither confirmed nor repealed. The Privy Council did not dignify it as legislation (*Acts P. C.*, Colonial, iv, 140, 809).

186. *Hite* v. *Fairfax*. The text of the stipulation, as recited in the report of the Lords of Trade, is as follows:
'And the Committee do further humbly Report to Your Majesty that the Petitioner the Lord Fairfax hath appeared in Person before this Committee and proposed and Consented that all the Grantees of Lands under the Crown within the Boundarys aforementioned shall quietly enjoy their Lands according to their respective Grants and likewise [has stipulated] to do and Consent to all such Acts as shall be thought necessary by Your Majesty to Confirm and Secure such Grantees in the quiet possession of their said Lands pursuant to their Grants and to Discharge Your Majesty from all Demands of the said Lord Fairfax on Account of Quit Rents that have been received by Your Majesty And to Yield up to Your Majesty all Arrears thereof that have hitherto become due; upon Express Condition nevertheless that the said Lord Fairfax shall for the future be entitled to all the Advantages Profits and Emoluments whatsoever to arise from Grants made by the Crown of Lands within his Boundarys, which the Crown would or might have been intitled unto by the Terms or in Consequence of the said Grants; and where, upon such Grants, Quit Rents are reserved, that he the said Lord Fairfax shall be intitled to Demand and receive the same from the Grantees to his own use and benefit from the time that Your Majestys Pleasure to be signified hereupon shall be made known to the Governor and Receiver General of Your Majestys Quit Rents in that Province.'
It was out of this stipulation that arose the celebrated cause, *Hite* v. *Fairfax*. Hite was the representative of a company of land speculators who had seated a number of families on the Shenandoah under orders of the Virginia Council made from 1730 to 1734 (*Va. Mag.*, xii, 115, 118; xiii, 120, 354). They returned surveys to the Secretary's office, but had not yet perfected Virginia patents before notice of the order of the Privy Council of 1733 suspended the activities of the Virginia government within the disputed bounds of the proprietary. When they came to his notice Lord Fairfax was moved to indignation by the Hite surveys, for he found them to be what would now be called 'shoestrings' or 'gerrymanders,' carefully laid out to include only bottom lands and so leaving the less desirable upland insulated and inaccessible to future seating. For this consideration in 1749 he refused to issue grants to Hite and his partners

until they should reform their surveys; whereupon they sued to enforce the decree of 1745. The proprietor's technical defense, formulated by the able Valley lawyer, Gabriel Jones, was based on the allegation that, lacking patents, Hite was not a 'grantee' within the purview of the stipulation of 1745. On this point the General Court held with the Hites in 1769 and 1771, and the defendant appealed to the Privy Council. The animosities of the original controversy having meanwhile died down, this appeal was not prosecuted; but, after Lord Fairfax's death, the Hites secured an affirmance of the judgment of the General Court by the Court of Appeals of Virginia, and so recorded (1786, 4 Call, 42) a mass of evidence for the early history of the Valley of Virginia.

The full record of the case, which was sent to England in 1772, survives in the British Museum (*Add. MS.,* 15317) and there are transcripts of the bill and answer in the MS. Division of the Library of Congress. That answer should be read by anyone interested in Lord Fairfax, for it is a mirror of his character.

187. See *Landmarks of old Prince William,* ii, 624.

188. So stated in a letter by George Fairfax to his brother, Bryan, March 28, 1783 (MS. *penes me*).

189. *George William Fairfax* (1725-1787), eldest son of William Fairfax and his second wife, Sarah Walker, was born at Providence in the Bahama Islands, January 2, 1724/5 (C. O., 23: vol. ii, 132). Taken by his father to Salem, he was sent thence in May, 1731 (Neill, *Fairfaxes,* p. 74), to be educated in England. There he remained until 1746, when, after a visit to Lord Fairfax at Leeds Castle, where he celebrated his coming of age, he returned to America and joined his father at Belvoir. It was as a consequence of this visit and the favorable impression then made that the proprietor wrote to his young kinsman on April 6, 1747 (Neill, p. 78), the announcement of his own impending arrival in Virginia, to which he added: 'I hope soon of having the pleasure of acquainting you of something to your advantage.' It is probable that this referred specifically to an appointment in the Customs service, but there can be no doubt that it expressed an interest and affection which persisted for many years and lead first to the appointment of George Fairfax as Agent for the proprietary and ultimately (when it appeared that the proprietor's brother, Robert, would leave no male heir and it seemed that the Fairfax title was to descend upon George) to a promise to make George the devisee of the interest in the proprietary itself, which by Fairfax's will eventually devolved upon Denny Martin. The evidence for such a promise is definite. Writing to his brother Bryan from England on March 28, 1783 (MS. *penes me*), George Fairfax said:

'I have only now to inform you that I have seen what is said to be a copy of the late Lord Fairfax's will and codicil, very different from what the good old gentleman voluntarily told me, with tears in his Eyes, when he did me the honour of a long visit previous to my departure last from Virginia—not that I am personally disappointed: but really am in respect to your children, that in all likelihood must bear an Ancient Title.'

It is altogether probable that Lord Fairfax altered his testimentary intentions partly because George had ceased to live in Virginia, but more for the reason suggested by this letter—that George Fairfax was himself childless.

At once upon reaching Virginia, in the spring of 1746, George Fairfax began his career. He represented his father in the arduous survey of the 'back line' of the proprietary, and was present at the planting of the 'Fairfax Stone' at the head spring of Potomac October 23, 1746. Soon thereafter he was included in the commission of the peace for Fairfax County. He sat in the Assembly of 1748-49 as a burgess for Frederick. During that session he married 'Sarah, eldest daughter of Col. Wilson Cary of Ceelys' (*Virginia Gazette,* December, 1748; *Sally Cary,* p. 23); and, his father's third wife Deborah Clarke being recently dead, established his wife at the head of the Belvoir household. He represented Frederick again in the Assembly of 1752-55, and his home county of Fairfax, in the Assembly of 1756-58. After his father's death in September, 1757, he declined to stand again for the House of Burgesses (Neill, p. 98); but used his interest to secure advancement to the Council. This he accomplished in May, 1767 (*Acts P. C.,* Colonial, v, 575; See also iv, 709), and in that capacity continued to participate in the administration of the Virginia government until 1773, when he finally left Virginia to reside in England (*Virginia Gazette,* June 24, 1773). Meanwhile he had served also other colonial offices. In 1755-56, he was Colonel of Frederick and organized the Rangers, which were then authorized by the Virginia government (Neill, p. 80; *Dinwiddie Papers,* ii, 248; *Journals H. B.,* 1752-58, p. 374). Before his father's death he seems to have been Collector of Customs for the Eastern Shore of Virginia (*Cf.* Neill, p. 91), but the Treasury Papers of the period relating to the customs are in too great confusion to confirm this, or even his appointment as Collector for South Potomac to succeed his father, which is amply proved by surviving correspondence.

Inheriting under his father's will, with Belvoir, the manors of Shannondale in Frederick [later Berkeley] and Piedmont in Loudoun, under a family entail he succeeded also, on the death of a paternal uncle, to the manor of Towlston in Yorkshire, where his father was born. This was the turning point of George Fairfax's life, for the responsibility of the English property called him to England in 1760 and again in 1773; and thus cost him not only the agency of the Northern Neck and his expected inheritance from Lord Fairfax, but the opportunity to take the part in achieving American independence which might fairly have been expected of his character and abilities. As it was, being at a distance, he was sympathetic but did not feel the fervor of the revolutionary sentiment, and so took no part. That he retained to the last the respect and affection of his life long friend, George Washington, is amply testified by their correspondence, which has been published among the letters by and to Washington. The most significant evidence for this is Washington's letter written to Robert Carter Nicholas when George Fairfax's American property was sequestered on the ground that he had become an alien enemy. Writing from 'Headquarters Passaic Falls, November 7, 1780' (*Writings of Washington,* ed. Ford, ix, 20) the Commander-in-Chief of the Revolutionary army in the field said:

'I hope, I trust, that no act of Legislation in the State of Virginia has affected or can effect the property of our good friend Colonel Fairfax, otherwise than in common with that of every good and well disposed citizen of America. It is a well known fact that his departure for England was not only antecedent to the present rupture with Great Britain, but before there was the most distant prospect of a serious dispute with that country; and if it is necessary to adduce proof of his attachment to the interests of America since his residence there, and of the aid he has given to many of our distressed countrymen in that Kingdom, abundant instances may be produced, not only by the Gentlemen alluded to in his letter of December 5, 1779, but by others that are known to me, and on whom justice to Col. Fairfax will make it necessary to call if occasion should require the facts to be ascertained.' This veto was, of course, effective.

During the last years of his life George Fairfax lived at Bath. There he died April 3, 1787, and was buried in the nearby parish church of Writhlington (See the MI. in *Sally Cary*, p. 7). His will is P. C. C. *Major,* 319.

190. Lacking the files of the *Virginia Gazette* of the period, the available evidence for the date of Lord Fairfax's return to Virginia is as follows: (1) On April 6, 1747, he wrote to George Fairfax from Leeds Castle (Neill, p. 78): 'I do not yet hear of any Convoy appointed for Virginia, but I hope soon to know of one being named that I may soon have the pleasure of seeing my friends in the Northern Neck.' A month later William Fairfax ceased to sign grants. (2) Another letter (Conway, *Barons,* p. 246), dated June 1, 1747, was evidently written in Virginia. (3) In August, 1747 (*N. N.,* F: 274) the Proprietor began in person to sign grants. (4) The *Maryland Gazette* of November 11, 1747, reported the return of the Governor of Maryland 'from Virginia, having been a journey thither on a visit to Lord Fairfax.'

191. The last grant signed by William Fairfax was dated in May, 1747 (*N. N.,* F: 269). The next succeeding grant, dated in August, 1747 (*N. N.,* F: 274), was signed by the proprietor.

It was because the proprietor was in residence at Belvoir at this time, as well as because that was the proprietary office, that the second state of the printed map of the Northern Neck designated the location of that house.

192. See George Washington's *Journal of a Survey,* 1748. The third member of the party was the Prince William surveyor, James Genn, who seems to have succeeded John Warner as the chief surveyor of the proprietary. He had been, with George Fairfax, one of the corps which located the 'back line' in the autumn of 1746; and is recited in *N. N.,* O: 72, as having made the original survey of the South Branch manor on March 31, 1747.

193. Neither in Fairfax nor Frederick counties was there recorded any procuration constituting George Fairfax the proprietary agent. The earliest evidence that he was acting in that capacity is the proprietor's letter of October 28, 1751 (Neill, p. 78). Following this there are several letters from Lord Fairfax of similar tenor, all prior to William Fairfax's death in 1757. The most definite is George's own letter to Governor Dinwiddie of September 4, 1755 (*ibid.,* p. 80), in which he excuses himself from an assignment to public service 'till I consult my good and indulgent Parent and my worthy Patron L'd Fairfax who, I am in hopes, will Spare me from his office.'

194. See the answer in *Hite v. Fairfax,*

195. George Washington's *Journal of a Survey*, 1748.

196. The earliest record of Lord Fairfax as a citizen of Virginia is in March, 1749, when he headed the list of trustees named in the act establishing Alexandria (Hening, vi, 214; C. O., 5: 1395, No. 20). Following this came the resolution of the Council on October 30, 1749, 'That a Special Commission issue to empower the Right Honourable the Lord Fairfax to act as a Justice of the Peace in all the Counties of the Northern Neck.'

The proprietor seems thenceforth to have voted regularly at all elections for burgesses throughout the proprietary, as he might under the law of the time in every county in which he was a freeholder; but Frederick became his bailywick. Whenever his residence was established there, he seems at once, in Governor Dinwiddie's phrase, to have been 'pleased to take the care of that county upon' himself; but it was not until September, 1754, when it had been demonstrated that the hardy individualists on the frontier would not enroll in the militia, that Dinwiddie sent to Lord Fairfax, with some apology, a formal commission to be County Lieutenant of Frederick. See *Dinwiddie Papers*, i, 48, 82, 312.

197. *N. N.*, H: 179. *Thomas Bryan Martin* (1731-1798) was the second surviving son of Lord Fairfax's sister Frances, who m. Denny Martin of Loose in Kent. In 1755 he was County Lieutenant of Hampshire, while his uncle served that office in Frederick. He sat in the Assembly of 1756-58 as burgess from Hampshire, and in that of 1758-61 as George Washington's colleague for Frederick. His name survives on the map of the Valley in the town of Martinsville, now W. Va. He died unmarried, leaving a will proved in the District Court at Winchester, October 1, 1798 (*Superior Court W. B.*, 1791-98, in Frederick clerk's office), which was subsequently interpreted in *Commonwealth* v. *Martin's executors*, 5 Munford (Va.), 117. Thereby he left the Greenway Court house and its contents to 'my present House keeper Betsy Powers and her heirs if she be alive at the time of my death,' with 1,000 acres surrounding it; but the remainder of his large landholdings he devised to his executors to be sold and the proceeds divided among his three surviving spinster sisters. As these ladies were resident in England and so aliens to Virginia the Commonwealth attempted to escheat Martin's lands, but unsuccessfully; for the Supreme Court ultimately upheld the plan of avoiding forfeiture which had been written into Martin's will by that able lawyer, Gabriel Jones.

198. Neill, *Fairfaxes*, 1869, p. 117.

199. *Ibid.*, p. 126.

200. *Ibid.*, p. 130. George Fairfax never forgave Martin for this. It was in resentment of it that after he had gone to England in 1773, and it was expected that Lord Fairfax must soon die, he fortified himself for retaliation by securing a procuration from Robert (later seventh Lord) Fairfax to resume the management of the proprietary as soon as it should devolve.

201. *Cf. N. N.*, I: 83, with K: 342, which respectively and contemporaneously record the earliest recitals of the Frederick office. It should be noted that beginning with a grant dated April 11, 1759,

Book I is countersigned, 'Examined per Thomas Bryan Martin' in respect of nearly every entry. This seems to indicate that Martin made periodical audits of the books at Belvoir on behalf of the proprietor.

202. *Robert, seventh Lord Fairfax of Cameron* (1706-1793) was the eighth and youngest child of Thomas, fifth Lord Fairfax, and his wife, Catherine Culpeper. Born at Leeds Castle, November 6, 1706 (the date is supplied by the Bromfield parish register, which also shows his baptism the following day), he grew up there. No record of his education survives, or, indeed, of any other activity of his youth until after the death of his second brother, Henry Culpeper Fairfax, in 1734; when, his eldest brother having given over the thought of marriage, Robert became, at the age of 28, heir presumptive to the family title and to the reversion of the estates in Kent and Virginia which were entailed under his mother's will. It was then that Lord Fairfax purchased for him a commission in the Horse Guards (The War Office record, 25: 89 *Commission Book* 1728-41, shows him Lieutenant, August 14, 1737, and Captain (exempt) July 21, 1739: he was later styled Major, but the commission does not appear). After Lord Fairfax returned from his first visit to Virginia and had determined to retire thence for the remainder of his life, he busied himself in establishing Robert as the resident representative of the family in England. First he had him returned to Parliament as burgess for Maidstone at the session of 1740 (he was returned again in 1747 in the same capacity, and in 1754 and 1761 as knight of the shire for Kent, but failed of re-election to the Parliament of 1767, *Official Returns of M. P.*, House of Commons Papers, 1878, vol. 62); and then arranged his marriage (April 25, 1741) to an heiress, Martha, daughter of Anthony Collins of Baddow, co. Essex, and niece of the banker, Sir Francis Child, Bart. (she died in 1747 and Robert married again in July, 1749, Dorothy Sarah, daughter of Mawdistley Best of Boxley, co. Kent, who died, *s. p.*, May 21, 1750). On his marriage he went to live at the Culpeper manor of Greenway Court in Harrietsham, near Maidstone; but upon Lord Fairfax's final departure for Virginia in 1747 he removed to Leeds Castle, where he spent the remainder of his long life.

When George Fairfax was in England in 1757 and again in 1762 he tried to persuade Robert Fairfax to go out to Virginia with him, urging (Neill, p. 133) 'it would be much to your interest to see once what must shortly be your property;' but it was not until the summer of 1768, after he had failed of re-election to Parliament, that Robert made the voyage (See the notice of his arrival in the *Virginia Gazette*, August 25, 1768). Thenceforth he appears often as a visitor at Belvoir in George Washington's diaries for the years 1768 to 1770, so that he must have spent several years in America. In 1775, however, he was again established at Leeds Castle (Neill, p. 164).

Robert Fairfax seems to have been willing to do what he could to secure to his cousins at Belvoir, out of the Culpeper inheritance, compensation for the alienation of the Fairfax estates in Yorkshire; but his own extravagant habits and the weakness of his character, which is revealed by his portrait, nullified this purpose. Indeed, the shoe was on the other foot: in 1785 George Fairfax wrote to his brother Bryan that he had been compelled to lend money to Robert on several occasions, until the calls on him be-

1781 Robert succeeded as seventh Lord Fairfax, being himself now seventy-five years of age. Under the terms of his mother's will he then, in his own right, became tenant in tail of Leeds Castle and of five-sixths of the Northern Neck proprietary. The Virginia estate, which was his principal expectation of revenue, had, however, by that time been sequestrated by the new Commonwealth and Robert, Lord Fairfax, was accordingly remitted for relief to the act of Parliament (28 George III, c. 44) passed for the relief of American Loyalists. His memorial to the commission created under that act was dated April 20, 1786 (P. R. O. Audit Office, 13: 28) and upon it he was allowed and paid £13,006, 8s. as the measure of his life interest in the proprietary (See Eardley-Wilmot, *Historical View of the Commission for . . . Claims of the American Loyalists*, 1815). This allowance was, however, swallowed up by Lord Fairfax's creditors so that when he died, July 15, 1793 (Bromfield Register; see also obituary in *Gentleman's Magazine*, August, 1793), he was in great straits: it was, indeed, recorded that 'this last nobleman after living in the most extravagant profusion, was buried in a manner more humble than the corpse of one of the meanest cultivators of his estate.' Robert, Lord Fairfax's, will was proved August 15, 1793 (P. C. C. *Dodwell*, 413) and merely confirmed his mother's testamentary dispositions, which he had no power to change, by devising 'to my nephew the Rev. Denny Martin Fairfax, D. D., all my manors etc., in Great Britain, America and elsewhere, and all my goods absolutely.'

203. Thomas, Lord Fairfax's will, dated November 8, 1777, and thereafter republished on October 5, 1778, and November 27, 1779, the last time with a codicil, was proved in Frederick Court May 5, 1782 (*Frederick W. B.*, 4: 583). The only reference therein to the Northern Neck was the following clause, viz:

'I give and devise all that my undivided sixth part or share of my lands and Plantations in the colony of Virginia, commonly called or known by the name of the Northern Neck of Virginia, with the several advowsons, and the right of presentations thereto belonging or appertaining, I have therein, with the messuages and tenements, buildings, hereditaments and all other appurtenances thereto belonging; all or any part whereof being formerly the estate of the Honourable Alexander Culpeper, Esquire, deceased; Together with all other lands and tenements I have, am possessed of, or have a right to in the said colony of Virginia, to the Reverend Mr. Denny Martin, my nephew, now of the County of Kent in Great Britain, to him, his heirs and assigns forever, if he the said Denny Martin should be alive at the time of my death:

'But in case he should not, then I give and devise the same and every part and parcel thereof to Thomas Bryan Martin, Esquire, his next brother now living with me, to him, his heirs and assigns forever; and in case of his death before me,

'Then I give and devise the same and every part and parcel thereof to my other nephew, Philip Martin, Esquire, brother to the aforesaid Denny and Thomas, and to his heirs and assigns forever,

'Provided always that the said Denny Martin if alive at the time of my decease, or in case of his death, the said Thomas Bryan Martin, if he should be alive at the time of my decease; or in case of both their deaths the said Philip Martin, if he should be alive at the Martin, Sibylla Martin and Anna Susanna Martin, and to each and every of them that shall be living at the time of my decease, an Annuity of one hundred puonds sterling during their and each of their natural lives and

'[*Provided*] *further* that the said Denny, or he to whom the said sixth part of the said Northern Neck shall pass by this my will, shall procure an Act of Parliament to pass to take upon him the name of Fairfax and coat of arms.'

Denny Martin (1726-1800), the eldest nephew here named, who was curate of Bromfield and Loose, co. Kent, survived Lord Fairfax, duly assumed the additional name of Fairfax, and in 1797 was confirmed therein by act of Parliament (37 Geo. III, Private, c. 33). In 1784 he went out to Virginia (See the recitals in *Hite* v. *Fairfax*, 4, Call, at p. 56) to assert his right and that of his uncle Robert to the proprietary under the Jay treaty of September, 1783, and by the caveats he filed against Virginia patents for Northern Neck lands (See in the Land Office at Richmond the book called *Caveats No.* 1, 1786-1814, pp. 51, 55, 56, 84, 86) precipitated the litigation reported as *Hunter* v. *Fairfax's devisee*, 1 Munford (Va.), 218; 7 Cranch (U. S.), 603; 4 Munford (Va.), 3; 1 Wheaton (U. S.), 304. In 1793, on the death of Robert, Lord Fairfax, he succeeded also, under the entail of Catherine Culpeper's will, to the full proprietary title and then at once sold out his claims to John Marshall, James M. Marshall and Raleigh Colston for £20,000. These purchasers negotiated with the Virginia Assembly in 1796 the settlement by which, in consideration of the waiver of the proprietary rights, 'the devisees of Lord Fairfax' were confirmed in possession of Lord Fairfax's manors (Shepherd, ii, 22, 140). Upon completion of the payment of the purchase money the final deed closing the Culpeper-Fairfax-Martin title was made October 15, 1806 by Philip Martin (1733-1821), the youngest nephew named in the sixth Lord Fairfax's will, who meanwhile under the entail and Denny Martin's will (P. C. C. *Adderley*, 596) had succeeded to the complete family interest.

The story of these proceedings has been admirably, and it would seem definitely, recorded by Mr. H. C. Groome in Fauquier Historical Society *Bulletin No.* 1 (August, 1921).

204. *Bryan Fairfax* (1736-1802) was the first child of his father's Massachusetts wife, Deborah Clarke, and in consequence was a half brother of George Fairfax. He was born in Westmoreland County August 11, 1736, two years after his father's arrival in Virginia (the date is supplied by George Fairfax's statement in the pedigree of the Towlston Fairfaxes, printed in *Harl. Soc. Pub.*, 1886, xl, 1295). While still a child, his father vested him with several land grants in what became upper Fauquier, aggregating 4699 acres, on Goose Creek and Little River (*N. N.*, E: 177, 281, 381; F: 55, 205). By reason of his mother's unwillingness to part with him during his tender years, he did not go to school in England, as did his brothers; but, after her death, was sent to be trained as a merchant in the counting house of one of his New England kinsmen at Barbadoes. At the end of several years' residence in the West Indies the 'place not suiting his Desires,' he secured his father's permission to return to Virginia in February, 1754 (*Historical Collections*, Essex Institute, 1880, xvi, 279). The next record of him is in the summer of 1756, when he was just twenty years of age. His father had proposed to 'strengthen my interest with the Secretary so as to give you

a clerkship in some good County when vacant,' pending which Bryan joined the Virginia regiment at Winchester as a volunteer cadet, at the moment when the military situation on the frontier was aggravated by the difficulties of securing drafts to recruit Washington's command. It was during this service that, while on exposed duty at night, he 'got religion' under circumstances which he subsequently rehearsed in a sermon (Neill, p. 175). On the reorganization of the regiment he was commissioned lieutenant of Capt. George Mercer's company and with it was stationed at Fort Cumberland for six months. In April, 1757, a disappointment in love ended his military career. While on leave he attended 'several merry meetings and dancings in Westmoreland and Essex' in the course of which he 'addressed' a young lady and was rejected. Without the knowledge of his father he then sent in a resignation of his commission under the impulse of a rash resolve to enlist under an assumed name as a 'private Centinel in some of the Northern Regulars,' and had gone as far on his way as Annapolis when his brother-in-law, John Carlyle, induced him to return home. He was then commissioned Captain of one of the two detached companies of Fairfax militia which were assigned to frontier service 'in hopes his courage and good conduct will give testimony of his capacity;' but before his company had seen any active duty the pressure of the indians was relieved and the militia was withdrawn. (For his brief military career see his father's letters in *Letters to Washington*, i, 251, 255, 264, 294, 297, 311, 332, 385; ii, 38, 69, 98, 108, 130; iii, 99; and other contemporary family letters MS. *penes me*.) His father died just after he came of age and he then found himself under the paternal will (*Fairfax W. B.*, B, No. 1, p. 171) in possession of the 5,568 acres of land in the Difficult Run neighbourhood of Fairfax County which William Fairfax had granted to John Colvill in 1739 and 1740, immediately purchased from him (*Prince William D. B.*, E: 207), and named 'Towlston Grange' after the Yorkshire house in which he was born. To this estate Lord Fairfax added in 1765, as a gift, his adjacent Great Falls Manor of 12,588 acres (*N. N.*, E: 38; I: 124. It was thus that the town of Matildaville came to be laid out in 1790 on 'land at the Great Falls of Patowmack in the County of Loudoun in the possession of Bryan Fairfax,' Hening, xiii, 171). Counting with these properties his original 5,000 acres in the piedmont, and as much more in the same locality which he soon inherited as heir at law of his younger brother, William Henry, who was killed with Wolfe at the capture of Quebec, Bryan was now vested with nearly 30,000 acres, much of which was already productive. This represented what was deemed an assured fortune: indeed, his successful brother-in-law, Robert Carter Nicholas, wrote him in 1763: 'I am, after a number of years fatigue possest of what you were born to.' On the basis of such a stake in the world he married, early in 1759, Elizabeth, daughter of Wilson Cary of Ceelys (See *The Virginia Carys*, 1919, p. 105), a younger sister of his brother George's wife, established himself at Towlston, and, being included in the Fairfax and Loudoun commissions of the peace (his portrait hangs among those of the colonial justices in Fairfax Court House), settled down to the life of a fox hunting planter and magistrate. During this period he cemented his boyhood intimacy with Washington, as is evidenced by their contemporary correspondence, by Washington's diaries, and, most of all, by the pleasant pictures of the Towlston household in the childish diary of his eldest daughter (See *Scribners Monthly*, 1876, xii, 301; *Sally Cary*, 1916). A characteristic lack of appetite for political leadership which was an anomaly in the previous history of his family, but persisted among his descendants, restrained him from accepting several invitations to be a candidate for the Assembly (*Cf.* *Writings of Washington*, ed. Ford, ii, 417; *Letters to Washington*, ed. Hamilton, v, 20); so that, outside of his steady service in the county court, the only public duties he now undertook were those of a trustee for the management of the 'great roads' leading from Alexandria to the Valley, under the act of 1772, and for the administration of the town of Warm Springs (Hening, viii, 547; ix, 247).

He was in England at the time of the passage of the Stamp Act, and both then and during the critical years after he had returned to Virginia resented vigorously the ministerial policy of coercion. Like most of his class in the colony he was weighed down by the burden of debt to British merchants which seems to have been the incitement to the development of Whig politics then in progress among the substantial planters; but when it came to revolution an obstinate sentiment of loyalty to the Crown aligned him with those who were unable to take the last step. He did not subscribe the non-importation agreement of 1770 and he earnestly sought to dissuade Washington from pursuing that policy at the time of the adoption of the Fairfax County Resolves of July, 1774. His argument was for reliance on petitions to the Crown, based upon the original Virginia charters; for he had heard from his brother George of the widespread sympathy with the position of the colonies among the gentlemen of Yorkshire. (See the original Association of 1770 with Fairfax County signatures among the Washington papers in the Library of Congress; and the correspondence of 1774 in Sparks, ii, 388, 488; *Letters to Washington*, ed. Hamilton, v, 22, 34, 121).

In the autumn of 1777, moved by a vain hope that by individual and personal representations to the ministry, supported by his family interest, he could bring about an understanding which might lead to peace, he determined on a voyage to England. On his way to New York to that end he was arrested at Lancaster, Pennsylvania, and, refusing to take a test oath, had the mortification to be incarcerated in the common jail until released on receipt of a pass from Washington, who then wrote, 'the difference in our political sentiments never made any change in my friendship for you, and the favourable sentiments I ever entertained of your honor leaves me without a doubt that you would not say anything or do anything injurious to the cause we are engaged in, after having pledged your word to the contrary' (See the documents printed in the *Richmond Standard* January 24, 1880). He accordingly pursued his journey to New York, but there again was unable to take the alternative test oath required by the British military authorities; and so was compelled to abandon a Don Quixote adventure. On his way back to Virginia he visited Washington at Valley Forge and soon after testified to his appreciation of their friendship in language which does credit to both: 'There are times when favors conferred make a greater impression than at others, for though I have received many, I hope I have not been unmindful of them: yet that, at a time when your popularity was at the highest and mine at the lowest, and when it is so common for men's resentments to run high against those who differ from them in opinion, you should act with your wonted kindness towards me has

ected me more than any favor I have received: and could not be
ieved by some in New York, it being above the run of common
ads' (See Sparks, v, 246). Thenceforth, like other Virginians
his class who held similar political opinions but were nevertheless
pected by the most ardent Whigs (e. g., William Byrd, Ralph
ormeley and Richard Corbin. See Eckenrode, *The Revolution in
rginia,* 1916, p. 126) he remained quietly at home during the re-
.inder of the war, suffering no molestation. It was after York-
vn and the sixth Lord Fairfax's death in 1781 that he had his
ortive experience as the last proprietary agent of the Northern
:ck.

The moral discipline of spiritual isolation during the Revolu-
n had stimulated in Bryan Fairfax a tendency to mysticism. Dur-
ʃ the remainder of his life his philosophy progressed from low
urch Calvinism, through the then novel evangelicanism to Sweden-
rgianism (See Bishop Meade, ii, 259, and the papers of Robert
rter of Nomini in the library of the New Church Theological
hool at Cambridge, Mass.). As a lay delegate to the Richmond con-
ntion in 1785 he was one of the organizers of the incorporated
iscopal church of Virginia (See the Journals of the church con-
ntions in the Appendix to Hawks, 1836), and in the following
ar was ordained a deacon by Bishop Seabury (Bishop Meade, *loc.*
.; Washington's *Diary*, July 27, 1786, recording a visit from 'Bryan
urfax, Esq., now Parson'). In 1789, on the death of the Rev.
ivid Griffith, (*Cf.* Hening, xiii, 312) minister of the churches in
nat had been Fairfax parish, he took priest's orders and thence-
rth, until 1792, officiated regularly at Christ Church, Alexandria,
d at Falls Church, though he would never accept 'the emoluments
the parish' (Bishop Meade, *loc. cit.*). When he resigned this
erical charge, Bishop Meade says the vestry 'entered on the record
. . the most flattering letter . . . regretting their loss of him.'
e now retired to 'Mount Eagle,' a house he had built in 1789 near
lexandria on a portion of John Colvill's estate, 'Cleesh' (See *Fair-
x D. B.,* R, No. 1: 365, 369; and the designation of the site of
[r. Fairfax's House,' which still stands, on Thomas' *Plan of the
own of Alexandria,* 1798).

Having survived both his elder brothers, Bryan succeeded as
ghth Lord Fairfax in 1793, but for several years 'he did not intend
king up his title;' which to him had now become a shadow. In
'98, however, he went to England to seek to recover some family
operty in Yorkshire, and while there was induced to change his
ind on the ground that the title 'may not in future be a disad-
intage to some of the descendants of your family.' The necessary
·oofs were accordingly submitted to the House of Lords. Mr.
Vykeham-Martin (*Leeds Castle,* 1869, p. 196) gives a touch of colour
› his appearance at this time: 'unlike the clergy of England his
·ess was a complete suit of purple in accordance with the custom
t Virginia.' On May 6, 1800, his place in the peerage was duly
ljudged (*Lords Journal*) but meanwhile he had himself returned to
irginia. It was thus that he was at 'Mount Eagle' on December
1799, when Washington 'dined at Lord Fairfax's,' on the last oc-
ısion when the Father of his Country went abroad for a social
isit (Washington's Diary in Ford, xiv, 242). He in turn dined at
[ount Vernon during the following week, but this was his final
wuch with his boyhood friend, for a few days later he was one of

the 'principal mourners' at Washington's funeral. (Washington's will, Ford, xiv, 286, recited, 'To the Reverend, now Bryan Lord Fairfax, I give a Bible in three large folio volumes with notes, presented to me by the Right Reverend Thomas Wilson, Bishop of Sodor and Man.' This Bible is now in the Library of Congress.)

Bryan Fairfax died at Mount Eagle on August 7, 1802 (*Baltimore Federal Gazette,* August 10, 1802. See his will dated May 18, 1793, proved September 20, 1802, in *Fairfax W. B.,* I, No. 1, p. 150; and the M.I. in Ivy Hill Cemetery, Alexandria). His first wife having died in 1778, he had married 2dly, in 1780, Jane, daughter of James Donaldson of Fairfax County (whose will, proved October 18, 1770, is recorded in *Fairfax W. B.,* C: 9) and left a daughter by her (See *Catlett* v. *Marshall,* 10 Leigh, Va., 79) as well as sons and daughters by his first marriage, from whom numerous progeny descend (See *Herald and Genealogist,* vi, (1870), p. 606). He was succeeded in the family title by his eldest son, Thomas (1761-1846), who lived out his life in Fairfax County, at first at Ash Grove on Difficult, and later at Vaucluse, near Alexandria (See *Scribners Monthly,* 1879, xviii, 715; Wormeley, *Recollections of Rear Admiral R. R. Wormeley, R. N.,* 1879; Harrison, *Recollections Grave and Gay,* 1911; and his will in *Fairfax W. B.,* U, No. 1, p. 382). From him descends the twelfth Lord Fairfax, who proved his title in the House of Lords, November 17, 1908, and has since sat as a representative peer for Scotland.

205. This procuration was not recorded in any county of the Northern Neck and no transcript of it has come to light but the tenor of it is proved by the letter of Robert, Lord Fairfax cited in the text, as well as in letters addressed by George Fairfax to his brother of dates April 15, 1782, March 28th and May 6, 1782, of which the MSS. are *penes me.*

The power, to which Robert Lord Fairfax referred, from Denny Fairfax to Bryan Martin and Gabriel Jones, authorizing them to co-operate with Bryan Fairfax in the administration of the proprietary and to join him in making deeds, was dated November 8, 1783, and remains of record in *Winchester Superior Court* D. B. 2: 23. But a congenital lack of sympathy between Bryan Fairfax and Bryan Martin doomed this arrangement to failure; with the result that to relieve the situation George Fairfax brought pressure to bear on Denny Fairfax by setting up back claims against the proprietary for uncollected commissions accrued, years before, to William Fairfax; whereupon, in consideration of the waiver of those claims, by a power of attorney dated September 21, 1784, Denny Martin revoked the authority of his brother and added his procuration to that of Robert Lord Fairfax (Cartmel, *Shenandoah Valley Pioneers,* p. 245). Thus Bryan Fairfax became sole agent.

206. The revolutionary proceedings of the Virginia Assembly with reference to the proprietary are in Hening, xi, 128, 160, 289, 543; xii, 111, 117, 239, 532. While accomplishing the destruction of the proprietary as an institution with the steady movement of a glacier, there was no radical temper shown by these acts. On the contrary the uniform respect they evinced towards the late Lord Fairfax himself suggests that had he been succeeded by another citizen of Virginia the property rights in the proprietary might have been preserved equally with those in the manors.

207. The papers relating to this claim are in P. R. O. Audit Office,

Class 13, Bundle 28. Lord Fairfax alleged that the proprietary was worth £4,000 per annum, which he capitalized at £98,000. It appears from Wilmot, *Historical View of the Commission for enquiry into the . . . claims of the American Loyalists,* 1815, that the Commission reduced this to £60,000 and in 1792 allowed Lord Fairfax £13,758, representing a commutation of his life estate. No provision was made for the remainder men.

208. By deed dated August 30, 1797, Denny Fairfax conveyed to John Marshall all his interest in the Northern Neck except Leeds manor, thus putting the grantee in position to carry out his bargain with the Commonwealth. After Marshall had completed the payments stipulated under the original contract of May 17, 1793, Philip Martin closed the transaction by a conveyance dated October 18, 1806, conveying to Marshall Leeds manor also. The conveyancing is discussed by Mr. Groome, from Fauquier records, in F. H. S. Bulletin, *loc cit.*

209. The last grant signed by Lord Fairfax was dated April 3, 1780, and was recorded in *N. N.,* S : 192. The first grant in the Commonwealth form, here recited, was dated November 15, 1786, and was recorded in the same book immediately following, at page 194. Thenceforth the series of Northern Neck Grant Books, as kept in the Commonwealth Land Office, was maintained through the alphabet, and, beginning a second series, proceeded to *N. N.,* G, No. 2. When that series was discontinued in 1862, all future Commonwealth grants were merged in a single record, which does not preserve the historical distinction between lands lying north and south of the Rappahannock.

210. This deduction was first made by Mr. Beer in *The Old Colonial System,* i, 194.

211. After the dissolution of the Virginia Company the Crown, by a series of patents, conferred the office of Treasurer of Virginia upon a succession of individuals, only one of whom (William Claiborne) was resident in the colony. None of those patents specified the privileges or obligations of the office; but it appears that all the patent Treasurers collected such quit rents as they could and retained them to their individual use, without accounting to the exchequer. See Howard Horsey's comment in September, 1636 (*Am & W. I.,* 1574-60, p. 302) that the Treasurer Jerome Hawley 'is lately dead, without giving any account of his service'; and Berkeley's report in 1671 (Hening, ii, 517) that 'there is no revenue arising to his majesty but out of the quit rents; and this he hath given away [in 1650] to a deserving servant, Col. Henry Norwood.' In a conversation with Frances Moryson in October, 1675 (Burk, ii, Appendix, p. xli), Lord Arlington confirmed this by the statement that he 'wondered why the country should be more aggrieved to pay him [Arlington] the quit rents [granted by the charter of 1673] than to Colonel Norwood and to others; since those rents had never been accounted for unto the chequer, but still received and enjoyed by the treasurers to their own proper uses.' It appears from various testimonies that after the Restoration Norwood registered his patent in the General Court and appointed resident deputies to exercise his function, but there is nothing to show what his actual collections were, except his own subsequent statement that they were irregular and did not represent the expectation of the rent roll. The difficulties Lord Culpeper had in collecting quit rents after 1673

are a familiar and often rehearsed record. Such was the situation in
May, 1680, when William Blathwayt was appointed Auditor General
for America and at once set about correcting the manifold abuses of the
colonial revenue. He procured the Commissioners of the Treasury to
call upon Col. Norwood to account for all quit rents received by him,
but was unsuccessful. Norwood argued, and maintained the position,
that the quit rents had been granted to him and that he had justly con-
verted them to his own use until they were granted to Lords Arlington
and Culpeper by the charter of 1673 (See Blaythwayt's *Journal*, 1680-.
1717, of which a full copy is in the *L. C. British Transcripts;* Cal.
Treasury Books, 1679-80, 1681-85, *passim*). It was only after the
surrender in 1684 of the charter of 1673 that Blathwayt was able to
organize a systematic collection and accounting for the Virginia quit
rents. For Blaythwayt and his energetic proceedings see Bond, *The
Quit Rent System in the American Colonies,* 1919.

212. In the MS. letter book (now in the Virginia State Library)
of William Allason, a merchant at Falmouth, covering the years 1760-
1800, there is preserved a general letter of instructions sent out by
Thomas Bryan Martin, agent for the Northern Neck proprietary, to his
'Collectors of Quit Rents,' under date of April 19, 1771, in which is
the following significant observation: 'The Quit Rents in the Northern
Neck and the Fines imposed by the County Courts therein have been
for some years so indifferently collected by the neglect of the Receivers
[that] the Arrears are become very considerable.'

213. *Acts P. C.,* Colonial, ii, 21.

INDEX

Commonwealth in land, origin of, 9; influence of Council in maintaining, 141; political consequences of successful fight to maintain, 137.
Connolly, John, 58.
Conway, Edwin, 106.
Corbin, Thomas, 98, 159.
"Corotoman," N. N. land office at, 93, 101.
Culpeper, Alexander, proprietor, 66; his will, 92.
Culpeper, Catherine, Lady Fairfax, proprietor, 78; her character, 97; her will, 101.
Culpeper, Margaret, Lady, proprietor, her will, 96.
Culpeper, Thomas, second lord, proprietor and governor, 33, 65, 68, 151; his death, 78.
Culpeper, Thomas of the Middle Temple, proprietor, 150.

Dale, Sir Thomas, governor, his "coming away," 14.
Dawkes, Henry, 43.
Deodands in N. N., 103, 161.
Dinwiddie, Robert, governor, his opinion of large land grants, 42; his proclamation of 1754 creating military rights, 54.
"Dividends" of land, origin of, 9.
Drayton, Michael, 42.
Dunmore, John, lord, governor, his land grants, 37.

Epes, William, 20.
Escheats, term of purchase of, 129.

Fairfax, Thomas, fifth lord, proprietor, 78.
Fairfax, Thomas, sixth lord, proprietor, 101, 105, 117, 169; his will, 171.
Fairfax, Robert, seventh lord, proprietor, notice of, 170; the devolution of N. N. title on, 117.
Fairfax, William, notice of, 162; his N. N. agency, 104.
Fairfax, George William, notice of, 166; his N. N. agency, 113.
Fairfax, Bryan, eighth lord, notice of, 172; his N. N. agency, 117.
Falmouth, N. N. land office at, 104.
Felgate, Robert, 142.
Filmer, Edward, notice of, 160; executor of Lady Fairfax, 101.
Fitzhugh, William, notice of, 157; his N. N. agency, 87; his "Ravensworth" grant, 70, 90.
Foote, Richard, 70.
Forts of 1646, military rights arising from maintenance of, 52.
Fox, David, 152.

Gates, Sir Thomas, his charter of 1606, 12.
Genn, James, 168.
George III, his proclamations of 1763 creating military rights, 57.
"Germanna," 147.
"Great Charter" of 1618, 15.
Great Meadows, capitulation at, 54.
Greenbrier Company, significance of land grant to, 54.
"Greenway Court," N. N. land office at, 113, 115.
Gooch, William, governor, his opinion of large land grants, 41.
Graffenried, Christopher de, 53.
Green, Charles, 116, 153.
Gregg, Thomas, 94.
Grymes, John, 103.

www.ingramcontent.com/pod-product-compliance
Lightning Source LLC
Chambersburg PA
CBHW062218080426
42734CB00010B/1932